The Walter Lynwood Fleming Lectures in Southern History

LOUISIANA STATE UNIVERSITY

THE SLAVERY DEBATES, 1952–1990

a retrospective

ROBERT WILLIAM FOGEL

LOUISIANA STATE UNIVERSITY PRESS   BATON ROUGE

12   11   10   09   08   07   06   05   04   03
5   4   3   2   1

DESIGNER: Barbara Neely Bourgoyne
TYPEFACE: Minion
PRINTER AND BINDER: Thomson-Shore, Inc.

I would like to thank the following publishers and organizations for their permission to republish excerpts from my previous works: the *Times Literary Supplement* ("From the Marxists to the Mormons," June 13, 1975), Stanford University Press ("Toward a New Synthesis on the Role of Economic Issues in the Political Realignment of the 1850's," in *American Economic Development in Historical Perspective,* ed. Thomas Weiss and Donald Schaefer, 1994), Editions Passé-Présent ("History with Numbers: The American Experience," in *Pour une histoire économique et sociale internationale: Mélanges offerts à Paul Bairoch,* ed. Bouda Etemad, Jean Batou, and Thomas David, 1995), The Civil War Institute at Gettysburg College ("The Quest for the Moral Problem of Slavery: An Historiographic Odyssey," 33rd Fortenbaugh Memorial Lecture, 1996), and W. W. Norton (*Time on the Cross,* vol. 1, 1989; *Without Consent or Contract,* vols. 1 and 2, 1989, 1992). In addition, this book includes extracts from my 1996 Charles Homer Haskins Lecture, "A Life of Learning," presented to the American Council of Learned Societies, and from *Time on the Cross,* vol. 2. I also want to thank Stanley L. Engerman for allowing me to use jointly written material.

LIBRARY OF CONGRESS CATALOGING-IN-PUBLICATION DATA:

Fogel, Robert William.
    The slavery debates, 1952–1990 : a retrospective / Robert W. Fogel.
        p. cm. — (The Walter Lynwood Fleming lectures in southern history)
    Includes bibliograpical references (p.   ) and index.
        ISBN 0-8071-2881-3 (alk. paper)
    1. Slavery—United States—Historiography. 2. African Americans—Historiography.
3. Racism—United States—Historiography. 4. United States—Race relations—Historiography. 5. Historians—United States—History—20th century. I. Title. II. Series.

E441.F625 2003
306.3'62'0973—dc21

2003009953

To Enid

My best friend and keenest critic
for more than fifty-four years

TABLE OF CONTENTS

PREFACE

Because these lectures are a personal, retrospective meditation on a series of debates that extended over most of my adult life, I have refrained from attaching the usual scholarly apparatus. I have freely drawn on my previously published research, and readers who want to know the sources for most of my views should consult those studies. A guide to the specific pages for relevant citations is contained in the acknowledgments. I have also drawn on the research and recollections of the numerous colleagues with whom I have collaborated, especially Stanley L. Engerman. Although quotations are not footnoted, the names of the individuals who made them are indicated in the text and the relevant publications are included in the references.

I am grateful to those who read and criticized various drafts of these lectures, including Allan G. Bogue, Dora L. Costa, David Brion Davis, Seymour Drescher, Stanley L. Engerman, Charlotte Fogel, Daniel M. Fogel, Enid M. Fogel, Henry Louis Gates Jr., Eugene D. Genovese, Mark Guglielmo, Farley Grubb, Richard Hellie, Michael F. Holt, Donald Lamm, Robert A. Margo, Peter Novick, Paul Paskoff, Orlando Patterson, Richard Sewell, Mark Smith, Kenneth Sokoloff, Richard Steckel, David Surdam, Howard Temperley, and Yasukichi Yasuba. I was also aided by comments made by audience members attending the 2001 Fleming Lectures at Louisiana State University. (My thanks to the Department of History and the university in general for their hospitality.) The final draft benefited from the editorial and analytical skills of Kate Hamerton and Susan Jones. Ms. (now Professor) Hamerton read all the drafts and made many insightful suggestions on both content and style. The successive drafts of the manuscript were patiently and efficiently typed by Donna Harden.

THE SLAVERY DEBATES, 1952–1990

Let me begin by defining what I mean by the slavery debates, since slavery has been debated for centuries. The slavery debates that I want to focus on are those engaged in by the generation of American scholars who came of age around the time of World War II. This war was critical because it unfolded under two competing scientific paradigms. The Nazis campaigned under the banner of the old anthropology, which held that there was a hierarchy of ability according to race, with Teutons at the top of the hierarchy and Africans at the bottom. The United States and its allies fought under the banner of the new anthropology developed by Franz Boas and his associates, which held that racial differences were superficial and that all human beings were essentially equal. It should be kept in mind that the United States, although it embraced the banner of racial equality, maintained a segregated army throughout World War II. It should also be remembered that segregation dominated American life at home. Schools, housing, restaurants, trains, buses, and occupations were segregated either by law, as in the South, or by a combination of laws, business practices, tacit agreements, and vigilante practices in the rest of the country.

It was this contradiction that was at the center of the debates about American slavery that unfolded after World War II. The principal participants in these debates were young scholars who had imbibed the new anthropology and were stirred by the determined efforts of returning black soldiers and other participants in the emerging black civil rights movement that gained new prominence with Martin Luther King Jr.'s inspiring 1963 speech on the steps of the Lincoln Memorial in Washington. Young historians were disturbed about the continued acceptance of racial stereotypes in the leading textbooks of the early postwar years and by the contention that slavery was merely a footnote to the main themes of American history.

There had been earlier challenges to these propositions, for the most part from black historians centered around the Association for the Study of Negro Life and History, founded by Carter G. Woodson in 1915, and its principal publication, the *Journal of Negro History.* Woodson wrote or edited eighteen books dealing with such diverse questions as the education of blacks during the antebellum era, the development of black churches, and the history of black wage earners. He was also an energetic and effective organizer who gathered around the association a large number of young, mainly black, scholars. Despite their methodological innovativeness in developing sources of evidence on the life and times of ordinary people and their effective demonstrations of the economic and social accomplishments of free blacks under conditions of adversity, their work was largely ignored by the mainstream white historians who dominated the historical profession through the early post–World War II years.

The debates that I am referring to, therefore, are the reconsiderations of the received "official" canon of knowledge on the nature of the American slave system, the conditions of slave life, and the moral problem of slavery that were launched by a young, postwar generation of American scholars. This canon was embodied in the work of Ulrich B. Phillips and other prominent historians often referred to as the "Phillips school." Phillips's most influential book, *American Negro Slavery,* was first published in 1918.

I date the beginning of the reconsideration with an article published in 1952 in the *American Historical Review* by Kenneth M. Stampp announcing his intention to write a book challenging the interpretations of U. B. Phillips and his followers. That book, *The Peculiar Institution: Slavery in the Ante-Bellum South,* was published in 1956. Although there were earlier calls for rewriting the history of slavery on the basis of the new anthropology, and although John Hope Franklin's erudite and comprehensive book *From Slavery to Freedom: A History of American Negroes* was first published in 1947, it was Stampp's critique of Phillips that shaped the debates over the nature of the slave system that unfolded during the next three decades. I choose 1990 as the closing date because by that year the post–World War II revisionism had largely run its course. In a dialectical process that would have pleased both Hegel and

Marx, lines of research previously considered incompatible had largely combined into a new synthesis. I do not mean to suggest that the history of slavery and its many ramifications is a closed subject. Quite the contrary, slavery research remains one of the most productive fields of historical literature in the United States and in other countries where slavery once thrived.

I cannot claim to be a detached interpreter of the huge literature that constitutes the slavery debates, because I was an active participant in them. Hence, although I have subtitled my lectures "A Retrospective," I want to emphasize again the personal nature of this retrospective.

In my view the slavery debates include not only the debates about how the slave system worked but also those about how the system was brought down and about the way in which the struggle to end slavery reshaped American civilization. My focus on United States slavery makes it difficult to do justice to the extremely rich body of work in recent decades on slavery in various other societies, including those of Latin America, the Caribbean, Western Europe, Russia, Africa, the Middle East, and the Far East. However, I draw on this research at various points in order to put the debates on American slavery into a broader perspective.

BREAKING AWAY FROM THE PHILLIPS TRADITION

It has been exceedingly difficult for revisionist historians to break away from the tradition initiated by Ulrich B. Phillips. Indeed, much of what I perceive to be the current consensus view of the relationships between masters and slaves and of the conditions of life under slavery is consistent with some of the main aspects of the Phillips interpretation, especially his description of the routines of economic life on large cotton and rice plantations. Although the new work condemns Phillips's racism, it recognizes that masters often had to compromise with the desires of their slaves, especially in providing considerable latitude to slaves in the use of their leisure time. The main breaks with the Phillips school have come in the redefinition of the moral problem of slavery, in the vast expansion of knowledge about the nature of slave culture, in the economic and demographic analysis of slavery, and in the integration of the history of the ideological and political struggle to end slavery with the new economic analysis of the system.

The Resilience of the Phillips Tradition

It might be supposed that the young, revisionist historians who had imbibed the new anthropology would have found it easy to break with the Phillips tradition. Phillips was, after all, so frank and unabashed in declaring his belief that blacks were a childlike, inferior race. At a time when such northern historians as James Ford Rhodes and John B. Mc-Master were damning the plantation magnates of the Old South for their cruelty and licentiousness, and even such ardent southerners as William P. Trent and William E. Dodd were upbraiding the masters for their arrogance, ruthlessness, and illiteracy, Phillips stubbornly defended their nobility. The masters of the great plantations, said Phillips, were "talented," "benevolent," and "well bred" men, who were "ruled by a sense of dignity, duty and moderation," who "schooled multitudes white and black to the acceptance of higher standards," and who "wrought more sanely and more wisely than the world yet knows."

To prove that his was the right view, Phillips set out to uncover evidence that would reveal the true nature of antebellum civilization. Whatever his motives, it was Phillips who launched the collection of systematic evidence bearing on the operation of the slave system. In so doing, he made a major contribution to the advance of American historiography in general and of southern historiography in particular. The data Phillips collected came from three main sources: records of large plantations, probate records, and bills of sale.

The plantation documents pertained to some sixty-odd plantations ranging in size from twenty-three to several hundred slaves, although most of them had in excess of one hundred slaves. In addition to cotton plantations in both the Old and New South, Phillips's sample included farms specializing in sugar, rice, tobacco, and general farming. Phillips did not compute fertility rates, death rates, or other key demographic variables. Nor did he systematically relate demographic characteristics to economic or social variables. He employed slave lists, mortality lists, clothing lists, and morbidity records in a rather informal manner, using them largely as ancillary support for impressions of plantation operations and life formed mainly from his reading of such plantation documents as diaries, letters, and instructions to overseers. It was on the basis of these varied sources of evidence that Phillips formulated his views of the annual work routine on large cotton, rice, and sugar plantations. Phillips also used this evidence as the basis for his characterization of the central features of plantation management and of the conditions of life for slaves.

Phillips's exploitation of the probate and sales records was more limited than his exploitation of the plantation documents. The evidence in these records was primarily numerical, and while Phillips had a greater appreciation of numerical evidence than most historians of his day, he does not appear to have been as comfortable with it as he was with literary evidence. Consequently his use of the probate and sales records was limited almost exclusively to the construction of indices of slave prices over the period from 1795 to 1860.

Whatever the limitations of his handling of the evidence he uncovered, the volume and quality of the records that he and his followers made available set a standard for historical research that his most severe critics have had to acknowledge and employ.

A second reason for the resiliency of the Phillips tradition is the way in which he embraced and worked within the *secularized* version of the indictment of slavery as it was shaped by the *Republican* party. I have emphasized the words *secularized* and *Republican* because the fundamental source of the campaign to abolish slavery was a powerful impulse in evangelical Protestantism that elevated doctrinal and ethical considerations far above material concerns. The religious radicals who sparked the abolitionist movement, convinced that they were divinely inspired, dismissed the dilemma that had beset the founding fathers between the natural right of the enslaved to their freedom and the natural right of the masters to the security of their property. Rejecting the rationalism of the Revolutionary generation, they denounced slavery as an unmitigated evil, incapable of being justified by material gain or any other worldly consideration. They declared that slavery was not just any sin but an extraordinary sin, a sin so corrupting that persistence in it, or complicity with it, infected every other aspect of life and created an insuperable barrier to both personal and national salvation.

Even the most devout abolitionists never relied exclusively on theological arguments, but until the end of the 1830s, the religious content of the appeal overwhelmed all of its other aspects. The publication of Theodore Weld's *American Slavery As It Is* (1839), which focused on the atrocities of slave owners, was the most visible sign of a shift to an appeal that was much more secular and political. This shift was quite gradual at first, partly because William Lloyd Garrison and other deeply mystical leaders resisted tactics that, however effective they might have been in attracting nonbelievers to the antislavery cause, would inevitably have corrupted the moral principles on which the movement was founded. Although the new secular arguments never entirely crowded out the religious ones, they overwhelmed the antislavery appeal fashioned by the Republican party after the mid-1850s.

The secularized Republican indictment of slavery turned on five main propositions:

1. that slavery was generally an unprofitable investment, or depended on trade in slaves to be profitable, except on new, highly fertile land;

2. that slavery was economically moribund;

3. that slave labor and agricultural production based on slave labor were economically inefficient;

4. that slavery caused the economy of the South to stagnate, or at least retarded its growth, during the antebellum era; and

5. that slavery entailed extremely harsh material conditions of life for the typical slave.

Phillips embraced the first four of these propositions without reservation, although he did not embrace the inferences that the authors of the indictment had drawn from them. The Republican indictment asserted that slaveholders had failed in a ruthless and immoral attempt to increase their wealth and income at the expense of those kept in bondage. But the first four propositions could also be used to support the hypothesis that Phillips favored. Phillips held that the main purpose of plantation slavery was not economic but social. In this view slave plantations were inefficient and unprofitable not because planters had failed but because efficiency and profit were not their central objectives—were not the criteria by which they evaluated the performance of the "peculiar institution."

To Phillips, the fifth point was the crux of the resolution of the conflicting interpretations. If it could be shown that the material treatment of slaves had been good by the standards of the day, if it could be shown that slaveholders had been paternalistic rather than ruthless, then his interpretation would prevail. His main efforts were directed toward documents capable of casting light on the relationship between masters and slaves. He found these in the records of large plantations. With the exception of the data on slave prices, Phillips's most noteworthy contributions to the fund of knowledge regarding the operation of the slave system came from plantation records.

These documents revealed that the food, clothing, shelter, and medical care provided to slaves were relatively good by working-class standards for the antebellum era. Methods of managing slaves turned out to be more complex and less harsh than suggested by most abolitionist tracts and by historians who uncritically accepted these tracts. Phillips also discovered more scope for an independent black role than the abolitionists had allowed. He conceded that masters had much power. But slaves, he argued, "were by no means devoid of influence." The regime that emerged was to a considerable extent "shaped by mutual requirements, concessions and understandings producing reciprocal codes of conventional morality."

The Phillips strategy was perplexing to many of the revisionist scholars, who thought that the key to unseating his intellectual dominion lay in disproving Phillips's idyllic description of plantation life. As it has turned out, this was a false scent. The key to superseding Phillips was in demonstrating that his first four points—the antislavery claims that Phillips built upon—were wrong. Slavery was repugnant, not because it failed to produce profits for the masters, but because it produced exceptional profits that served to prolong an immoral system. Slavery was repugnant, not because it caused the southern economy to stagnate, but because slaves were excluded from the benefits of rapid economic growth. However, in the 1950s, conceding the vitality of the slave economy seemed to many, if not most, of the revisionists to be the wrong way to overturn the Phillips tradition and to clear the way for a history of slavery based on the new anthropology. The hesitancy to reject such a large part of the Republican indictment of slavery contributed to the durability of the Phillips tradition.

Still another reason for the durability of the Phillips tradition was the particular difficulty that many revisionists had with the proposition that slavery was economically moribund and soon would have expired without the necessity of a Civil War. To reject that proposition, to say that the slave South was highly profitable and growing rapidly, seemed to be falsely celebrating an immoral system. But neither did they wish to concede that the Civil War was an unnecessary blunder because slavery was on the verge of economic collapse and self-destruction. One cautious response was that planters were so blinded by their ideology that they failed to recognize that they were using their resources inefficiently and hence refused to consider a peaceful abolition of slavery. However, the claim that a class that had produced such brilliant politicians as Washington, Jefferson, Madison, Jackson, and Calhoun and far more super-rich magnates than the North, could not perceive its own best economic interests, was difficult to sustain.

Hence, for the most part, the anti-Phillips revisionists avoided the issue. Because they were stymied by the proposition that slavery was moribund, the revisionists found it difficult to confront the claims of the Phillips school that the master class was more dedicated to a way of life than to economic aggrandizement; that it was merely trying to preserve the virtues of agrarian life and all that went with it—closeness to nature, self-sufficiency, leisure, human relations, and family—from the onslaught of an aggressive urban industrialism that promoted a "cash register" mentality and threatened old virtues.

The Impact of The Peculiar Institution

It was not until the publication of Kenneth M. Stampp's *The Peculiar Institution* that a successful assault on the Phillips tradition was launched. Interestingly, Stampp rejected much of the abolitionists' economic indictment of slavery. The "critics of slavery who argued that the institution was an economic burden to the master," said Stampp, "were using the weakest weapon in their arsenal."

Although Stampp's incisive critique of the economic indictment is one of the best chapters in his book, it is also one of the least mentioned. Descriptions of *The Peculiar Institution* more often stress its depiction of slavery as "a thoroughly cruel and brutal system of social control," as "primarily a harsh, repressive system for the exploitation of cheap labor," and as "the most bestial regime that has tarnished America." Except for the cliometricians, revisionists paid little attention to the chapter that focused on the issues of profit, economic viability, efficiency, and economic growth.

Stampp's book concentrated on the issue of the treatment of slaves. There was virtually no defense of the behavior of the slaveholding class put forward by Phillips that Stampp permitted to pass unanswered. Where Phillips pleaded that slave owners had inherited the system,

Stampp replied that "they built it little by little, step by step, choice by choice." Where Phillips characterized slaveholders as men of goodwill whose treatment of slaves was generally "benevolent in intent and on the whole beneficial in effect," Stampp responded that "cruelty was endemic in all slaveholding communities" and even those "concerned about the welfare of slaves found it difficult to draw a sharp line between acts of cruelty and such measures of physical force as were an inextricable part of slavery." Where Phillips lauded the bountifulness of the food provided to slaves, Stampp countered: "On countless farms and plantations the laborers never tasted fresh meat, milk, eggs, or fruits, and rarely tasted vegetables."

Perhaps Stampp's most important contribution was his unremitting assault on racist depictions of blacks. The agenda of the stereotypes to be demolished was, once again, provided by Phillips. Stampp pursued this agenda relentlessly. He first attacked the basic racist premises that governed Phillips's characterizations of slaves. Against the belief that blacks were biologically inferior to whites, Stampp pitted "an impressive accumulation of evidence" by "modern biologists, psychologists, sociologists, and anthropologists" that "Negroes and whites have approximately the same intellectual potentialities." Against the belief that personality and temperament made blacks "the natural slave of the white man," Stampp argued that variations in the "personalities of *individuals* within each race are as great as the variations in their physical traits. Either slavery was a desirable status for some whites as well as for some Negroes, or it was not a desirable status for anyone."

When it came to the issue of black cultural identity, the problem that confronted Stampp was not that Phillips had denied American blacks a distinct culture but that he had made the innate and immutable inferiority of blacks the source of a distinct culture defined by such characteristics as "cowardice," "docility," "proneness to superstition," "submissiveness," "inertness," "humble nonchalance," "licentiousness," and a proclivity for "lying," "shirking," and "stealing."

To counter Phillips on these points Stampp embraced the theme of the "day-to-day resistance" which had been popularized by the anthropologist Melville J. Herskovits and his students Raymond and Alice Bauer. Rather than challenging Phillips's contention that lying, stealing, shirking, and feigning illness were the characteristics of slave behavior, Stampp affirmed that they were. The question became not the appropriateness of Phillips's description of the behavior of slaves but the proper interpretation of the significance of this mutually agreed upon description.

Stampp's line of argument permitted the issues of racism to be confounded by a debate over value judgments. To Phillips the "good" slave was the one "who was courteous and loyal to his master, and who did his work faithfully and cheerfully." But in a system as evil as slavery, Stampp contended, normal ethical standards did not apply. In such a system the "good" slaves were those who "faked illness, loafed, sabotaged." Indeed, Stampp made this precept part of the moral code of slaves. "For appropriating their master's goods they might be punished and denounced by him, but they were not likely to be disgraced among their associates in the slave quarters, who made a distinction between 'stealing' and 'taking.'" Quite the contrary, the "generality of slaves believed that he who knew how to trick or deceive the master had an enviable talent, and they regarded the committing of petit larceny as both thrilling and praiseworthy."

Whatever was wanting in slave culture, Stampp argued, was due to the dehumanizing nature of the slave system rather than to race. Thus, if slaves exhibited a tendency to violence, it was because of "the brutalizing effect of bondage." If slaves had a "casual attitude" toward marriage, if husbands and wives failed to develop "deep and enduring affection" toward each other, it was because of "the general instability of slave families" promoted by the system, because of the forced "disintegration" of African "social organization," and because of the "easy access to female slaves" by marauding white males.

A world in which good work is synonymous with betrayal and in which evasion, deception, and sabotage are the objectives to which to aspire leaves scant room for black achievement. Stampp did acknowledge some positive achievements under adversity, including the acquisition of some labor skills, the development of a folklore and folk music, and the shaping of some distinctive religious rituals. Nevertheless, he emphatically rejected the proposition that slaves could have developed a truly independent and articulated African American culture because they lacked the political power and institutional instruments to do so. Hence, they lived in a "kind of cultural void," in a twilight zone "between two cultures."

That was about all that could be expected from a system in which cruelty and violence toward slaves were endemic. For Stampp, cruelty arose not because of the malevolent nature of the slaveholders but because of the malevolent nature of the system—because a master could brook nothing less from his slave than "perfect" submission. To achieve that goal, masters were impelled, regardless of their humanity in other respects, to develop in the slave "a paralyzing fear of white men," to "impress upon him his innate inferiority," and to "instill in him a sense of complete dependence." While Stampp did not employ the concentration camp analogy later set forth by Stanley M. Elkins, his plantation strongly suggested a prison with cruel wardens.

Although *The Peculiar Institution* was coolly received by the elders of the historical profession, it was enthusiastically embraced by the young revisionists. By the mid-1960s it superseded Phillips as the standard interpretation of slavery in the antebellum era. The profession finally had a history of slavery based on the new anthropology.

Rediscovering Achievement under Adversity

Although a return to a history based on the old anthropology was unthinkable, events outran the reign of *The Peculiar Institution*. The rise of a powerful and highly successful civil rights movement stimulated a desire to reconsider the history of slavery and to expand the legacy of achievement under adversity so skillfully developed in the writings of Carter Woodson, John Hope Franklin, and other black historians. The search for the existence of a distinct and well-articulated black culture under slavery led scholars to reconsider what was positive and useful in the work of Phillips. A generation of historians firmly committed to the new anthropology found it possible to look past the racist aspects of Phillips's works and to find the existence of a well-articulated, distinct, and creative African American culture in the body of evidence he supplied. Hence, the new focus on the rise and development of black culture under slavery is still another factor that has impeded a break with the Phillips tradition.

The turning point came in 1966 with the publication of a foreword by Eugene D. Genovese to a reprinting of Phillips's *American Negro Slavery*. In that foreword Genovese excoriated Phillips for his racism but praised his recognition "that slavery 'was less a business than a life.'" Genovese acknowledged that Stampp had struck numerous blows against Phillips's racism but accused Stampp of misunderstanding the complexity of the relationships between masters and slaves, a complexity that Phillips, for all his racism, had grasped. With his Marxian appetite for contradiction and synthesis, Genovese called attention to those passages in *American Negro Slavery* that stressed the mutual interdependence of masters and slaves. He praised Phillips for recognizing that the plantation system was shaped by mutual requirements of masters and slaves that led to reciprocal concessions, understandings, and codes of behavior, which made the impact of slaves on the personality of the master as profound as that of the master on the personalities of the slaves. This theme, which was extended a few years later in an article published in the *New York Review of Books*, culminated in *Roll, Jordan, Roll: The World the Slaves Made*.

A similar point about the nexus between masters and slaves was made by David Brion Davis, when he related a story about the Greek philosopher Diogenes of Sinope. After his slave ran away, Diogenes said that his slave could live without his master, but his master could not live without his slave. Later, when pirates captured Diogenes and took him to a slave market, he pointed to a rich spectator and said, "Sell me to *this* man; he needs a master." The point, said Davis, was that although the servant was the instrument of his master's will, the master's identity required a slave who recognized him as master. Since such recognition required an independent consciousness, the relationship between master and servant could always be reversed. In dealing with slaves down through the ages, masters were forced to recognize their fundamental humanity and make suitable accommodations.

As scholars subsequently delved into the work regime of slaves, they discovered sharp limits to the power of masters, who felt constrained to recognize the customary rights of their slaves. Such scholars as Genovese, Sidney W. Mintz, Douglas Hall, and Philip D. Morgan pointed out that although these rights were not recognized by law, failure to respect them could undermine the productivity of slaves. So masters often had to offer "overtime" pay or other compensations to elicit labor. Even more startling was the discovery of an independent slave economy within the plantation regime. In the South, as elsewhere in the New World, slaves used their spare time to grow their own crops and sell them, to acquire capital, and to act as entrepreneurs.

Parallel to the rediscovery of the hidden slave economy was the rediscovery of a resilient slave family. The new view of the slave family was portrayed in a series of books and papers published in the 1970s and 1980s by John Blassingame, Genovese, Herbert Gutman, Cheryll Ann Cody, Elizabeth Fox-Genovese, Barbara J. Fields, and Jacqueline Jones, among others. Using autobiographies of runaway slaves, interviews with former slaves in the 1920s and 1930s, and plantation records, these scholars found not only that slaves were deeply devoted to their families but that, despite the pressures of the slave trade, most slave households were headed by two parents, most slave children were raised in such households, and fathers exercised a far stronger role within the family than some scholars had assumed.

Despite elements of consensus on the work patterns of slaves and the resiliency of slave families in the face of many negative pressures, attempts during the 1960s and 1970s to reconstruct slave culture raised more issues than they solved. Particularly vexing were disagreements about the "autonomy" and "uniformity" of slave culture. The term autonomy refers to the degree to which slaves produced a distinctive slave culture that was independent of white influences; uniformity refers to the degree to which slaves shared common views and responded in similar ways to the various aspect of their lives, their circumstances, and their physical and spiritual futures.

Investigators of slave culture generally agreed that the culture that arose among slaves was an adaptive response to their circumstances. Since their circumstances were to a considerable degree shaped by white masters and overseers, all the scholars acknowledged at least the indirect influence of whites on this culture. The disagreements on autonomy turned on the extent to which slaves were able to choose which aspects of white-imposed technology, skills, attitudes, and values they would accept. Disagreements on autonomy also involved the extent to which slave culture incorporated elements that were drawn from sources other than the European heritage of whites—from either their African heritage or those spontaneously invented by slaves as a result of the circumstances under which they lived.

Historians of slave culture also generally agreed that regardless of the idiosyncrasies of individual masters, local customs, and local laws, most slaves shared some elements of an African heritage, accepted various elements of Christianity, valued kinship, and sought varying degrees of independence from their ubiquitous and powerful oppressors. They agreed that the common experience of oppression and African heritage were not by themselves sufficient to provide all slaves in the New World with a common culture. The material and social circumstances that served to shape slave culture varied over both space and time. Household organization, language, planter policies, policies of religious and secular authorities, demographic factors, conditions of labor, slave social structure, the extent of contact with whites, and the extent of direct contact with Africans were so different from one slave colony to another—such as Cuba, Jamaica, the Bahamas, Haiti, or Surinam—that they produced quite different slave cultures in the various colonies despite the common African heritage and the common oppression experienced by all slaves in the New World.

Disagreements about the uniformity of slave culture included such issues as the intensity of carryovers of African culture and whether African heritage, except in a highly attenuated sense, could have provided slaves with a unifying cultural outlook, since the ethnic groups of Africa from which the slaves were drawn were differentiated from each other by a myriad of languages, religions, and customs as well as by a variety of political and economic institutions. A critical issue for historians of the South was the extent of the spillover of the cultural norms that developed on the minority of plantations with such large numbers of slaves that the hands lived out their lives mainly in a black world (having little contact with their white masters) and were (within certain sharply defined limits) largely self-governing. How could the culture developed on such large plantations have been transmitted to the majority of slaves who lived on relatively small plantations, which usually had fewer than five slave households and in which hands generally worked alongside their masters?

During the 1970s and 1980s, scholars of slave culture stressed the many difficulties that arose from the types of evidence with which they were forced to work. The publications, the private letters, and the other papers of slaveholders "can hardly be accepted as 'objective,'" wrote Genovese, "especially when they purport to describe slave attitudes." He also noted the limitation of such other white sources as the accounts of travelers to the South, which, even when they were not written by persons with axes to grind, "varied considerably" with the "talent, length of stay, and social attitudes" of the writers. Nevertheless, Genovese, Blassingame, and the other scholars in the forefront of research on slave culture continued to make use of these sources (just as W. E. B. Du Bois and Franklin Frazier had done in their classic studies of the slave family decades earlier) because, as Genovese put it, "no comprehensive treatment can afford to ignore them."

Perhaps the greatest advance in the reconstruction of slave culture was the systematic utilization of black testimony, which prior to the 1970s had been largely neglected. Blassingame assembled and carefully studied the published autobiographies of runaway slaves because they represented "the largest body of life histories dealing with the intimate details" of slave life, and because they revealed "what went on in the minds of black men." Genovese was more skeptical of this source than Blassingame. He argued that even when these autobiographies were not strongly influenced by the abolitionists who edited them, they remained "the accounts of highly exceptional men and women and can be as misleading in their honesty and accuracy of detail as in the fabrications."

Although Genovese made use of the fugitive autobiographies, he favored the interviews with thousands of ex-slaves conducted in the 1920s and 1930s, first by scholars at Fisk University and Southern University and later by the Federal Writers Project of the Works Progress Administration (WPA). He and some other scholars believed these interviews are a better source of information about slave life than the autobiographies of the runaways, not only because they are more numerous, but also because they represent the broader slave population. Whatever their advantages, the interviews remain a less-than-perfect source of evidence. In the edition of over 2,300 interviews published by the Greenwood Publishing Company in 1972, for example, residents of the state of Arkansas provide nearly 30 percent of the interviews, although that state had less than 2 percent of the slave population in 1850.

The preponderance of whites among the interviewers also troubled some scholars. Blassingame suspected that the ex-slaves were more reserved in speaking to white interviewers and may even have given misleading replies to some questions. The age of the ex-slaves at the time of the interviews is another possible source of bias. With two-thirds over age eighty when interviewed, it is possible that time had dimmed memories of the harshness of their experiences. Blassingame suggested that ex-slaves who managed to live to such ripe ages might have been better off than the majority of slaves. Some argued that superannuated slaves who were interviewed during the depression of the 1930s would have looked back favorably on the security of slavery. Others believed that the narratives may confuse the memories of slave and postemancipation experiences.

Spirituals and folklore are a third major source of black testimony about life under slavery. According to Sterling Stuckey, the study of folk material provided an effective way of getting "'inside' slaves to discover what bondsmen thought about their condition." A similar point was made by Lawrence W. Levine, who argued that folk materials refuted the view that slaves were "inarticulate intellectual ciphers." Folk materials, he continued, showed that slaves were "actors in their own right who not only responded to their situation but often affected it in crucial ways." Levine, who worked his way through thousands of black songs, folktales, proverbs, aphorisms, jokes, verbal games, and oral narrative poems, was keenly aware of their limitations as a historical source: dates, locations, and creators of folk materials were hard if not impossible to determine; some folklore was censored by editors, while other offending materials were banished completely, neither published nor preserved; and the black narrators "were often extremely selective and circumspect in choosing the songs and stories they related to the dignified whites" who came to collect them.

Whatever the category of slave testimony, two points are commonly emphasized by the scholars who have worked on these documents: one is the potential pitfalls of this type of evidence; the other is a confidence in their ability to cope "with altered documents, with consciously or unconsciously biased firsthand accounts, and with manuscript collections that were deposited in archives only after being filtered through . . . overprotective hands." According to Genovese, an experienced investigator can tell what is and what is not typical, what does and does not ring true. Thomas L. Webber argued that "although it would be extremely difficult to make an adequate analysis of the life or character of any individual slave" from the material in his or her autobiography or interview, "a satisfactory analysis" of the culture of the slave quarter "as a whole can be achieved when the sources are studied in their entirety." Virtually all of the scholars working on slave culture during the 1970s and 1980s agreed, as Genovese put it, on the need to "weigh different kinds of testimony against each other," feeling safest in their conclusions "when various kinds of sources" tended "to agree on what, how, and where, even if they disagree on interpretation and value judgment."

New Directions in the Study of Slavery

Although the new work on slave culture has gone far beyond the thought of Phillips, it is not an unambiguous break with the Phillips tradition. A much clearer break is to be found in Phillip D. Curtin's *The Atlantic Slave Trade: A Census,* which was published in 1969. Not only did this book integrate African studies with southern studies and put U.S. slavery in a global perspective, it also pushed demographic and epidemiological issues to the forefront of attempts to describe and evaluate population changes. As a result, explanations for the differences in the rate of growth of particular slave populations were freed of the shackles created by the slave-breeding hypothesis, which was invented by Theodore Weld and reinvigorated by Stampp and by some cliometricians. Influenced by Curtin's book, subsequent studies, making use of large data sets that had languished in British, Dutch, French, Portuguese, Spanish, and Scandinavian archives, linked variations in vital rates of slaves to particular crops, time periods, geographic characteristics, and household characteristics. The surge in comparative studies of slavery made it clear that sugar, rather than cotton, was the driving force in the Atlantic slave trade. The development of an increasingly sophisticated understanding of sociology and anthropology revealed variations in plantation regimens from one society to another and, within particular societies, by crop. Such knowledge laid the basis for comparing similarities and differences in slave culture all across the Americas. One of the most revealing of the comparative studies of slavery was Orlando Patterson's *Slavery and Social Death: A Comparative Study,* which discussed the internal dynamics of slave systems in sixty-four societies, from ancient times to the mid-twentieth century.

The ability to view Phillips in a new light was facilitated by the sudden intrusion of a large corps of economists into the slavery debates during the 1960s. This intrusion was welcomed by neither the defenders of the Phillips tradition nor the neoabolitionist school led by Stampp. The cliometricians, as they were called, refused to be bound by the established rules of engagement, and they blithely crossed ideological wires in a manner that perplexed and exasperated traditional historians on both sides of the ideological divide. Yet they opened an important and enduring new page in the slavery debates.

Cliometrics is the systematic application of the behavioral models of the social sciences and their related mathematical and statistical methods to the study of history. There were isolated attempts to develop this approach in historical work before the Second World War, but it was not until the late 1950s that these coalesced into a sustained intellectual movement. By 1960 cliometric bridgeheads were established in economic, social, and political history. The bridgehead expanded most rapidly in economic history where, within the space of a decade, one-time Young Turks were transformed into a new component of the establishment.

The decade of revolution began with an article entitled "The Economics of Slavery in the Ante Bellum South," written by Alfred H. Conrad and John R. Meyer, who were then young assistant professors at Harvard University. While this highly technical article attracted little public notice, it touched off one of the longest and most passionate debates in the discipline of economic history and stimulated the entry of a large group of fledgling economists eager to participate in a crusade to extend the movement for quantification from the social sciences to the humanities. The result was an outpouring of work aimed at a "scientific" reinterpretation of the slave economy.

The intrusion of cliometricians into the slavery debates complicated them by raising highly divisive issues about the appropriateness of using quantitative methods in a humane discipline. The use of statistical tools in historical research is now so widely accepted it is hard to believe that efforts were once made to keep it at bay. Yet no new trend in the writing of history was more bitterly or more frequently denounced in the 1960s and 1970s.

Viewed in retrospect it is clear that the verbal battles between cliometricians and traditional historians during the 1960s and 1970s were nothing less than a cultural war. C. P. Snow raised the specter of war in his Rede Lecture, *The Two Cultures and the Scientific Revolution*, which was published in 1959. Simultaneous careers as a scientific administrator and novelist made him acutely aware of the extent of the breach that had developed between the humanities and the sciences. In his view, humanists and scientists formed not only two vocational groups but two distinct cultures. The men who made up these cultures, though of comparable intelligence and social origins, were so far apart in intellectual, moral, and psychological assumptions that they had ceased to communicate. They "had so little in common," said Snow, "that they might have inhabited different worlds."

Although such alienation made a war predictable, the battleground was surprising. The war erupted in history rather than in some no-man's land between physics and literature. It was not provoked by the elders of history. Theirs was a humane discipline that sought little, and could gain little, from the sciences. The task of historians was to serve as the creators of tradition. The challenge to them resided not so much in the mastery of the facts, although that was an important part of the work, but in the reworking of the facts into narratives that transmitted high culture and fundamental values in a manner more gripping and more intriguing than fiction. Their heroes were not physicists but poets. The critical skill was not statistics but imagination. Do not "succumb to the dehumanizing methods of social sciences," said Carl Bridenbaugh in his Presidential Address to the American Historical Association, and do not "worship at the shrine of that Bitch-goddess QUANTIFICATION."

The address was delivered in December 1962. It was a cry aimed at rallying younger scholars against barbarian invaders who had by then made deep inroads into their territory. It is common to date the birth of cliometrics to the presentation of the slavery paper by Conrad and Meyer five years earlier. The difficulty is with the metaphor. Cliometrics was not "born." It gradually emerged from a complex set of developments in the social sciences, in history, and in applied mathematics, much of which had already taken place before World War II. By the early 1950s young historians and historically minded social scientists at many universities were experimenting with the applicability of quantitative methods to a wide range of historical issues. So by the time Conrad and Meyer delivered their slavery paper, there was a substantial audience for it.

I was a graduate student at Johns Hopkins in 1958 when the slavery paper was published. The debate in our department raged for weeks and embraced most of the graduate students and faculty of economics. Some were elated by this attempt to extend "hard" scientific methods to a central question of American history. I found it difficult to believe that a system as reprehensible as slavery was so profitable and along with others searched for analytical errors that would overturn the finding. The only important error discovered in that effort, when corrected by Yasukichi Yasuba, who later became a distinguished development economist at Osaka University, actually reinforced the conclusions of Conrad and Meyer by showing that the profitability of slavery was not only high but increased rapidly during the last two decades of the antebellum era.

If the paper by Conrad and Meyer generated electricity among economists, it drew lightning bolts from traditional historians. Genovese took time out from his work on *The Political Economy of Slavery* to attack this cliometric sortie into his field. Not only had the two economists mauled the data, he charged, but they were extremely naïve in their interpretation of the politics and culture of the master class. "If cliometricians were asked to write a history of the crucifixion," he said later, "they would begin by counting the nails."

Those who had acquired a command of quantitative methods were euphoric and as unbounded in their praise of the power of the new techniques as they were critical of traditional ones. During the early 1960s a few cliometricians, such as David Landes, then at Berkeley and a few years older than most of his fellows, called for more modest claims of accomplishments and stressed the line of continuity between the new work and the old, but the euphoria was too powerful to be contained.

Among the innumerate historians the reaction was quite different. C. Vann Woodward, the doyen of southern history, who later did much to heal the breach between cliometricians and traditional historians, originally saw cliometrics as a "cult" dominated by "zealots" whose language "strained the limits of polite intercourse" and whose "aggressive posture" and "philistinism have thrown some of our more conservative historians into a state of shock." Still more serious was the condition of innumerate graduate students, spoken of protectively by Woodward as "our young." During the mid-1960s he noted "among them a mood of incipient panic, a mounting fear of technological displacement, and a disposition among a few to rush into the camp of the zealots." To counter the panic Woodward and other elders sought to assure their students that there was plenty of history to be written that did not require quantification. They also set out to develop "a small cadre" within their own ranks that would be so well "armed with all the weapons, trained in all the techniques, and schooled in the ideology of the invaders" that they could expose the "sophistries" and "pretensions" of the aliens.

The entry of the cliometricians into the slavery debates was indicative of a general growth of scholarly interest in the subject. A search of the terms "slavery," "antislavery," "abolition," and "slave trade" in the online catalog of the Library of Congress for the period 1940–1989 revealed an explosive growth in books on slavery in the 1960s and 1970s. A similar search in *American History and Life* and *Historical Abstracts* revealed a comparable explosion in journal articles on slavery. Several new specialist journals came into being to accommodate the outpouring of research, but many of the articles appeared in more general journals.

By the early 1970s, the new findings of slavery research began to be reported in journals aimed at intellectuals generally. Reviews of scholarly books on slavery began to appear regularly in such publications as the *New York Review of Books,* the *New York Times Book Review, Time, Newsweek,* and sometimes even in *Esquire.* Some slavery books became the lead reviews and provoked discussion and debate throughout the academy. The wide interest in the new findings on slavery and the intensity of some of the scholarly debates attracted the attention of newspapers across the country and around the world. Television talk show hosts began to interview slavery historians, and in 1977 the miniseries based on Alex Haley's *Roots* became a blockbuster. Although public interest in slavery research has abated somewhat, scholarly interest has continued to expand. The annual number of articles on slavery published in scholarly journals during the last decade of the twentieth century was at an all-time high.

COMING TO TERMS WITH THE ECONOMIC
VIABILITY OF SLAVERY

The cliometricians were odd entrants into the slavery debates. None of them were specialists in Southern history. Many were not even economic historians; those who were specialized in the traditional topics of economic historians: manufacturing, transportation, trade and commerce, banking, agriculture, fiscal policy, labor, and technological innovation. My dissertation and my first two books were on railroads. Stanley Engerman's dissertation was on fiscal policy. Our first joint publication was on the iron and steel industry. Roger Ransom's dissertation and first publications were on canals. Paul David worked mainly on problems of technological change. Peter Temin's first book was on the iron and steel industry. Richard Sutch was not originally an economic historian: his dissertation and early articles were primarily on monetary policy. Alfred H. Conrad and John R. Meyer were primarily econometricians, with Meyer specializing in investment theory and urban economics and Conrad in problems of fiscal policy. Among the cliometricians who figured prominently in the slavery debates of the 1960s and early 1970s, only Gavin Wright and Claudia D. Goldin had dealt with the slave South in their dissertations.

Cliometric Techniques and Issues

The cliometricians were primarily interested in applying the behavioral models of the social sciences and their related mathematical and statistical methods to the study of history. It was natural for Ph.D. students in the social sciences to think of using the required tools of their discipline to analyze not only contemporary problems but those of the past as well. The fields of history that most obviously lent themselves to the new methods included economic history, demographic history, urban history, parliamentary history, and the history of popular voting behavior. Since quantitative methods were more effective in describing the characteristics of large groups of people than individual behavior, they were especially useful to historians who wanted to study the history of ordinary people. Methods of analysis and types of information that are appropriate for determining whether Thomas Jefferson's income declined during the postrevolutionary years are not appropriate for determining whether the income of American farmers as a class declined or rose, which requires information on the frequency distribution of the many incomes in that class. Although quantitative methods are not the only way of dealing with groups, they facilitate the exploitation of sources of information that could not otherwise be analyzed.

Cliometricians have worked out rules for processing quantitative evidence that are akin to the rules worked out a century and a half earlier by German historians of ancient and medieval societies for the study of languages (philology), writing (paleography), documents (diplomatics), seals (sphragistics), and coins (numismatics) and for the identification of medieval and ancient weights. Cliometric procedures pertain to such matters as the authentication and verification of both quantitative and testimonial evidence, the correction of incomplete or otherwise unrepresentative data sets, the use of sensitivity analysis to determine the effect of errors (in either the data or the analytical apparatus imposed upon the data) on the conclusions drawn from the analyses, and the use of simulation models to evaluate the information content of patchy evidence. Five decades of experience in applying these procedures provide ample testimony to their value in historical work.

Cliometric techniques have also been applied to issues in European history. The methods of family reconstitution developed in France by the demographer Louis Henri and in England by historians E. A. Wrigley and Roger Schofield made it possible to reconstruct the course of mortality, fertility, and nuptiality going back to 1740 in France and to 1544 in England. Analyses based on these data made it possible to trace the rise of fertility control, first by the regulation of the age of marriage and then by contraceptive methods within marriage. Peter Laslett reconstructed the social structure of households in England during the early modern era and compared them with households elsewhere in Europe. Related cliometric techniques made it possible to trace the escape from hunger and high mortality in Europe and America between 1750 and the present, revealing the key roles played by the expansion of the food supply and the revolution in public sanitation. Cliometric reconstructions of fertility, mortality, and nutritional status are beginning to provide reliable answers to the long debate over how a millennium of cycles of overrapid population growth followed by chronic malnutrition and deadly epidemics was brought to an end.

It was the methodological challenge posed by Conrad and Meyer's 1958 paper on slavery rather than the substance of the issue that initially caught the attention of most of the cliometricians. The central problem posed by Conrad and Meyer was one of logic, not ethics: it concerned the inferences about profitability that could validly be drawn from the data needed to compute a rate of return. When the debate among cliometricians pushed beyond the bounds of economic logic, it initially went no further than questioning the empirical validity of the estimates of the economic and demographic variables employed by Conrad and Meyer. During the 1960s the investigation of the economics of slavery was extended to include two additional issues: the economic viability of slavery and the rate of economic growth in the antebellum South. During the 1970s the cliometric research on slavery was extended to the measurement of the relative efficiency of free and slave farms, to the economics of urban slavery, to the demography of slavery, to the nutritional assessment of the slave diet, to the analysis of the characteristics of slave families, and to a number of other cultural issues.

In their effort to resolve these issues, cliometricians brought large amounts of new evidence, mostly but not exclusively quantitative, into play. These included large samples drawn from the manuscript schedules of U.S. censuses, from probate records and invoices of slave sales, from the registration records of slaves in the British West Indies and in the Dutch colonies, from the ex-slave narratives, from military records, and from British, French, Dutch, Portuguese, Scandinavian, and Spanish records on the slave trade. The data in these sources were not only costly to retrieve and to process but were extremely difficult to work with. It required a good deal of research to evaluate their biases and to devise procedures to make effective use of them. The issues raised by the work of Conrad and Meyer on profitability, for example, were not resolved for nearly two decades despite the large number of cliometricians participating in the debate.

During the decade of the 1970s, the growing mountains of evidence finally made it obvious that the profitability of slavery was increasing, not declining, on the eve of the Civil War. Moreover, the sharp rise in the purchase price of slaves relative to their rental price meant that slave owners were never more confident about the future of their system than they were during the last half of the 1850s. By the 1970s still another issue was settled by the reworking of the national income accounts for each state. Far from stagnating, the per capita income of the South was growing faster between 1840 and 1860 than that of the North. The relative efficiency of slave agriculture was the last of Phillips's issues to be investigated by the cliometricians. The research disclosed that slaves working under the gang system produced as much output in thirty-five minutes as farmers—white or black—produced in an hour when working in the traditional way. It was an ominous finding. Cliometricians were initially deeply divided on the plausibility of research that made an evil system so productive. The finding was also initially condemned by many social and political historians because it seemed to imply that slaves had collaborated in their own oppression. The debate on the relative efficiency of slave agriculture raged throughout the late 1970s and 1980s, but it too was resolved by new evidence and new analyses that confirmed the initial finding.

The process by which cliometricians progressed in their reconsideration of the central points in the abolitionist indictment is well illustrated by the evolution of the debate on the profitability of slavery. Virtually every important point in the original essay by Conrad and Meyer, from the equations they used to calculate the rate of return on investments in slaves to the estimate of each variable they employed in the calculation, was challenged by one critic or another. A succession of theorists contributed to the refinements in their basic equations, eventually bringing into them terms that more accurately reflected the mortality and fertility rates of slaves as well as a number of costs and revenues not originally taken into account. A succession of empiricists designed new, larger, or more representative samples of data to replace the limited ones that Conrad and Meyer found in secondary sources. Among the fruits of this work was the sample of five thousand southern farms employing forty thousand slaves, randomly selected from the 1860 census by William N. Parker and Robert E. Gallman, which led the way in exploiting the new power of computers for historical research. Other new data sets collected by other investigators included samples of prices and hire rates of over 100,000 slaves of all ages (from infancy to past eighty) who lived between 1700 and 1865 and information on births and deaths that were obtained from probate records, census schedules, and a sample of plantation account books from across the South, some of which contained information on up to five generations of slave families. Each harvest of new data called forth a new, more accurate formulation of the equations describing the relations among the variables. Each reformulation of the basic equations pointed to the need for more or different bodies of data. In this process the divergent views gradually gave way to a general consensus.

Thus, in an abstract way cliometric research conformed to the conventional model of how to conduct scientific research in history: detached, unemotional, respectful of fellow investigators. In practice this model of behavior broke down. Even as the weight of evidence accumulated on successive points, establishing increasingly solid findings, differences of opinion on particular results and procedures mounted and tensions became acute.

Despite the cliometricians' desire to develop a precise, emotionally detached, ideologically neutral analysis, moral issues unavoidably intruded into cliometric discussions. At one conference, for example, a cliometric debate over the appropriate adjustment for cluster sampling (sampling by counties instead of by individual plantations) became so emotional and explosive that it startled the traditional historians. "So," said one of these onlookers privately, "I see that you cliometricians can also become ideological."

It was not the technical aspects of cliometrics that led to such emotional episodes but the discomfort and embarrassment that cliometricians felt when attempting to measure rates of return on men, women, and children or to compute efficiency indices for a morally corrupt system. Few could escape the feeling that even at a distance of more than a century the dirtiness of the business was rubbing off on them. And those who were coming up with results that showed slavery to be more profitable and efficient, or less lethal, than it was portrayed in the abolitionist indictment labored under the fear that not only the quality of their research but also their personal integrity would be called into question. The "most unfortunate aspect of the discussion," said John R. Meyer in a letter commenting on a meeting held midway through the twenty-year debate on the profitability of slavery, was

> the notion that if one insists upon a fairly precise quantitative evaluation of the business aspects of slavery then one is guilty of "lacking heart" or otherwise being insensitive to the very human losses and sufferings involved in slavery. A very strong implication in much of the discussion was that Conrad and I were guilty of such insensitivity; this was, needless to say, rather thoroughly upsetting to us. Perhaps the strength of my reaction was overdone. Nevertheless, I ask others to place themselves in our position: how would you react to listening to one hour of fairly substantive implications that you lack sensitivity to the race issue?

Measuring the Relative Efficiency of Slave Labor

The anxiety and divisiveness caused by the debate over the profitability of slavery was only a prelude to the emotional storm that greeted the effort to measure the relative efficiency of slave and free labor in agriculture. When Engerman and I embarked on this project in 1968, we assumed that we could dispense with this issue quickly. Since a long list of public figures, historians, and economists, dating back to Benjamin Franklin and Adam Smith, had argued that slave labor was quite inefficient, and since this view was in varying degrees embraced by all of the reigning historians, we had little reason to doubt that this was the case.

Early in 1968, Engerman and I decided to measure just how much less efficient southern slave agriculture was than the northern system of free family farming. The project seemed straightforward. Economists had for some time been working on the problem of how to compare the relative efficiency of two economies or two sectors of the same economy. In this connection they had devised an index (called "the geometric index of total factor productivity") that was relatively easy to compute. We did not feel that we needed a very precise version of this index. Something that gave us a rough idea of the relative level of the inefficiency of southern agriculture was good enough. For such a task, we thought, the data on agricultural production in the published census of 1860 would do. The whole enterprise could be completed in a few weeks.

The result of the crude index was quite odd. It showed that southern agriculture was 9 percent more efficient than free northern agriculture—an absurd result. We had been too cavalier; we had allowed ourselves too many assumptions we knew to be untrue in order to reduce the burden of work. So we began working on the evidence needed to make a number of adjustments we had previously passed over. One was an allowance for the fact that southern livestock were generally much lighter than northern livestock. We also recalibrated the labor inputs (to take account of the higher proportion of women and children in the slave than in the free labor force) and the land inputs (to take account of the difference in the average quality of northern and southern land). To our surprise, the adjustments went in the wrong direction: the relative advantage of slave agriculture *rose* from 9 to 39 percent.

This startling result jolted us into the realization that we, as well as most previous students of the antebellum South, might have seriously misconstrued the nature of that economy. We had to confront the discomforting reality that, although American slavery was deeply immoral and politically backward, it might, nevertheless, have been a highly efficient form of economic organization that was able to sustain high rates of economic growth and yield substantial profits to its ruling class.

Still, the result did not sit well with us and we did not rule out the possibility that we had fallen into some unsuspected analytical trap. Our instincts continued to resist the implications of our findings. How could a system so impoverished in labor skills be efficient? How were the masters and the overseers able to overcome the indisputable sluggishness of the slave labor force, whether this sluggishness was because slaves had been reduced to Sambos, as Stanley Elkins believed, or because of their resistance to exploitation, as Kenneth Stampp argued. How could one account for the peculiar dichotomy under which slave labor apparently was quite efficient in an agricultural setting but by all accounts so inefficient in the city that urban slavery was on the verge of collapse?

With research support from the Ford Foundation and the National Science Foundation, Engerman and I began the search for the massive amount of data needed to resolve these issues. The information sought was of such staggering proportions that, had we been confronted with the task of compiling all of it from scratch, we might well have faltered in our resolve. Fortunately, a major effort to collect data bearing on the slave economy had been initiated in the early 1960s by Parker and Gallman. By 1968 Gallman and Parker had not only succeeded in retrieving a random sample of five thousand farms and forty thousand slaves from the original handwritten schedules compiled by the census takers in 1860, but they and their students had used the sample to estimate the pattern of southern food consumption, to compare the productivity of large and small farms, and to describe the distribution of wealth. The work of Gavin Wright, who showed that the Parker-Gallman sample could also be used to measure the advantage of large-scale plantations, was particularly illuminating.

We drew on the experience of two other former students of Parker and Gallman: James Foust, who had been the chief assistant to Gallman in retrieving the sample from the manuscript schedules and in coding the data for the computer, and Fred Bateman, who had written a thesis under Parker on the dairy production of both northern and southern farms. Foust and Bateman agreed to undertake the task of collecting and coding a sample of twenty thousand northern farms. Engerman and I were thus free to concentrate on the search for the additional southern data needed to supplement the Parker-Gallman sample.

We began a systematic canvass of southern archives in January 1971, hoping that the two of us could complete the task of data collection within a year. That turned out to be a vain hope. After four years of work, with the aid of more than thirty research assistants, the task of collection was still incomplete, even though we had accumulated information on more than 250,000 slaves. It was this enormous store of data—not only many times larger, but also much more systematic than that previously available—that permitted the reinterpretation of slavery set forth in *Time on the Cross*. In order to make the reinterpretation accessible to general readers, we summarized the initial findings in a primary volume and reported the data and analytical procedures on which the reinterpretation was based in a companion volume. That two-volume study, intended to be a preliminary report that would be refined in subsequent research, was published in 1974.

The public debate set off by the publication of *Time on the Cross* greatly accelerated the pace of research on the economics and demography of slavery. It was a debate in which there were no losers. The detailed scrutiny of our preliminary findings pointed up numerous gaps that required additional data or different analytical techniques and broadened the range of issues under investigation. Much of the debate was focused on the three questions that had been at the center of cliometric work on slavery before 1974 and were also central topics in *Time on the Cross:* the profitability and economic viability of slavery, the rate of southern economic growth between 1840 and 1880 and the factors that influenced it, and the relative productivity of slave and free agriculture. Not only was there a searching reexamination of the conceptual bases for many of the earlier computations, but many aspects of the operation of slave markets and of antebellum agriculture, commerce, and manufacturing were more deeply probed than ever before. New bodies of relevant data were uncovered that made it possible to estimate variables and parameters bearing on aspects of the slave economy that previously had to be left to conjecture. Although the new work did not dramatically revise the basic estimates of profitability, the rate of southern economic growth, or the relative productivity of slave agriculture that were reported in *Time on the Cross,* it produced a far more detailed and textured picture, not only of the nature of the slave economy and the forces that influenced its development but also of the free economy.

Consider, for example, the way in which the debate over the length of the work year of free farmers and slaves served to extend knowledge about the operation of both labor systems during the antebellum era.

The issue arose when initial efforts to compare the productivity of free and slave farms revealed that the latter were more efficient. This unexpected result raised questions about the way in which the labor input had been measured, particularly about the decision to measure the labor input in man-years rather than in man-hours. The plausibility of the criticism touched off an extensive search for data bearing on the length of the northern and southern work years, and on labor schedules generally, in order to determine if the hypothesized difference in annual work hours could account for the differences in measured productivity.

The results of the effort to test the hypothesis about work schedules were surprising and highly informative. As it turned out, free northern farmers worked about 10 percent more hours than southern slaves, not fewer hours as had been hypothesized. Specialization in livestock and dairying not only led to longer workdays than specialization in crop production but also increased the number of hours worked on Sundays. The principal reason for the longer work year in the North than on slave plantations was that the North specialized in livestock and dairying, but on the large slave plantations hardly 5 percent of output originated in these activities. The new data revealed other unsuspected features of the slave mode of production, such as the highly regular pattern of days worked per week (and hours worked per day) over the seasons. It soon became evident that the greater intensity of work per hour, rather than more hours of labor per day or more days of labor per year, was the principal form of the exploitation of slave labor. The gang system played a role comparable to the factory system or, at a later date, the assembly line, in regulating the pace of labor. It was, in other words, an early device for speeding up labor.

The implications of these discoveries about work schedules have not yet run their full course. They coincide with new discoveries about manufacturing that have led to a wide-ranging reconsideration of the initial phases of the Industrial Revolution. New hypotheses have been formulated that emphasize not mechanization and labor saving but the more efficient exploitation of the existing labor supply as the principal result of the factory system. More particularly, it is argued that factory technology was designed to make use of forms of labor, particularly the labor of women and children, that could not be as effectively employed as the labor of adult males in certain agricultural contexts. According to this hypothesis, the relative effectiveness of women and children in the production of raw cotton inhibited the growth of the factory system in the South, while the inability of grain farming to effectively exploit such labor spurred the factory system in the North. These and other new hypotheses have led to a deeper search for the information locked away in previously examined censuses and factory reports and to searches for new bodies of data capable of revealing the sources of increased productivity in the early factories and for data bearing on the relationship between factory growth and the relative productivity of women and children in agriculture.

The most dramatic new cliometric findings since 1974 have to do with the health and demography of slave populations, which were still infant subjects when we dealt with them in *Time on the Cross.* No other fields of slavery research have grown more explosively than these have, and the sophistication of the investigations in demography, nutrition, and general biomedical knowledge has grown apace. The analysis of immense bodies of demographic and anthropometric data for slave populations in the United Sates, the British West Indies, Cuba, Brazil, and various ethnic groups in Africa became feasible as the cost of data processing declined. These developments have produced better explanations of both the high fertility rates of U.S. slaves and the differences between their fertility and mortality rates and those of the slave populations in the Caribbean and South America.

The breakthrough on health and demographic issues was spawned largely by the attempt to test the abolitionist charges that slaves were severely malnourished. In *Time on the Cross* we sought to address this issue by making use of data in the Parker-Gallman sample of the manuscript schedules of the U.S. census for 1860 to estimate nutrients available for consumption by slaves on large plantations. There were, however, numerous questions raised about our data sources and estimation procedures, as well as about the inferences that could be drawn from our findings.

That debate helped to stimulate an intense search for other types of data bearing on the slave diet. Stephen C. Crawford turned to the ex-slave narratives (interviews of former slaves conducted in the 1920s and 1930s) and found information that enabled him to characterize the diffusion of various foods among slaves as well as the association between the variety of the diet and such matters as plantation size and the opportunity of slaves to supplement the master's ration. Archaeologists and medical anthropologists investigated the remains of fauna in excavations of the slave quarters of twenty plantations in five states. Economic and social historians searched plantation records, legal records, prison records, and similar documents for information either on actual consumption or on rations specified in orders to overseers or in public decrees.

Information on diet only reveals nutrient intake (gross nutrition) and by itself still leaves open the issue of whether a given diet was adequate to sustain rapid physical development and good health in the face of heavy claims on the diet. Consequently, some investigators turned to height and body mass indices, which are measures of net nutrition, to assess the nutritional status of slaves. Others searched journals for reports of nutritional diseases among slaves and analyzed frequency distributions of causes of death for clues about the prevalence of nutritional deficiency diseases.

The new data not only made it possible to resolve points that were at issue in the mid-1970s but revealed aspects of slave nutritional status and health that were not even contemplated during these debates. It now appears that children rather than adults were the principal victims of malnutrition. Despite the fact that they were worked quite hard, the relatively good health of adolescent and adult U.S. slaves is reflected in their mature stature, their high body mass indices (a measure of weight adjusted for height), and their life expectancies. In order to sustain their heavy levels of work, adult slaves were relatively well fed, clothed, and housed. Much of the new story turns on the overwork of pregnant women, which diverted nutrients from the development of the fetus. As a consequence slave mothers typically produced small babies, which, even if not neurologically impaired, were vulnerable to infections that sturdier infants could have survived. Infant death rates were exceedingly high, running about 30 percent, and partly because of poor weaning diets, about 20 percent of the survivors died between ages one and five.

Contributions to the Reconstruction of Slave Culture

Cliometricians also contributed to the reconstruction of slave culture by destroying the myth of the incompetent black worker, a myth originally put forward by apologists for slavery but later carried forward by neoabolitionist historians who promoted the theme of "day-to-day" resistance or argued that slavery had reduced slaves to Sambos.

The difficulties created for these views of the slave work performance and ethic by the new findings on the productivity of slave labor are immediately apparent. Slave plantations and laborers were not less efficient than free farms and free farmers. Slaves on small plantations who, like ordinary hired hands, worked in the fields alongside their masters were just as productive as free farmers. But those who toiled in the gangs of the intermediate and large plantations were on average over 70 percent more productive than either free farmers or slaves on small plantations. These gang laborers, who in 1860 constituted about half of the adult slave population, worked so intensely that they produced as much output in roughly thirty-five minutes as did free farmers in a full hour.

That gang laborers were harder working and more productive than their free counterparts did not, of course, rule out the type of behavior that has been called day-to-day resistance. But it did raise questions as to the extent of this behavior and its location. Not all large plantations were as successful as the average and it might have been that the types of sabotage of production described by Melville J. Herskovits and Stampp were heavily concentrated on the less successful plantations. Plantations run on the gang system might have been sabotaged, even though they were more productive than free farms, if they fell well below the standard for the gang system.

But even if day-to-day resistance was rife on the more brutal and presumably less successful plantations, one should not blithely translate resistance into low labor performance. Resistance could reduce but not cancel out the greater intensity of gang labor. Resisters who were able to deprive masters of half the extra product to be expected from the gang system (it would be a rare plantation on which sabotage was that effective) would still have found themselves compelled to produce as much output in roughly forty-five minutes as did free men in a full hour. In other words, while sabotage could have deprived the master of some of his gain, it could not free the slaves from the burden of intense labor. And there was a heavy price to be paid for this type of resistance. On plantations where stealing was most frequent, masters made heavier use of the lash, provided coarser diets, and imposed greater restrictions on freedom than were typical of paternalistic plantations.

Genovese proposed an alternative way of reconciling the resistance work ethic with the new findings on slave productivity in *Roll, Jordan, Roll.* He argued that large slave plantations represented "a halfway house between peasant and factory cultures" and that planters sought to impose a factorylike discipline on their labor force. On the other hand, he insisted that while slaves were willing to work extremely hard, so hard that they could "astonish the whites by their worktime élan and expenditure of energy," they would do so only sporadically, and they resisted efforts to subjugate them to the tyranny of regularity, to transform them into "clock-punchers." "The actual work rhythm of the slaves," then, was "hammered out as a compromise between themselves and their masters."

This modified view of resistance overcame several of the difficulties in the thesis it sought to replace. The perpetual sabotage movement embodied in the concept of day-to-day resistance was, as a general phenomenon, incompatible with the findings on productivity. The high level of productivity implied either that such resistance failed dismally, over and over again, or that it was so limited in extent and localized that it left aggregate production largely unaffected. Genovese replaced the image of slaves in a perpetually unsuccessful campaign of sabotage with one in which slaves strove to modify the most distasteful aspects of the system in ways that would ameliorate their oppression. Slaves worked hard but extracted concessions. Masters attempted to exploit these concessions for their own purposes but, under slave pressure, ended up making "far greater concessions to the value system and collective sensibility of the quarters than they intended." In this world in which frontal assaults were suicidal but successful struggles for amelioration of the worst abuses were possible, an ethic which embraced hard work and was responsive to economic inducements was not necessarily an act of collaboration or a sign of weakness of character. While reformist rather than revolutionary, such behavior emerged as a significant form of struggle for the interest of the slaves. Genovese's thesis preserved the notion of slave resistance and even allowed for substantial success of limited goals while at the same time making slave behavior consistent with high levels of productivity.

However, his sharp distinction between the regularity of factory production and the seasonality of plantation production was overdrawn, especially for the antebellum era. Many blast furnaces, for example, especially those using charcoal, operated for only part of the year. And textile production, milling, transportation, meat packing, and various other industries tracked by economic historians exhibited sharp variations in levels of production over the seasons.

Nor was the seasonality of labor demand as uneven on plantations as Genovese suggested. His insistence that heavy labor requirements were limited largely to a short period at harvest time drew too heavily on the experience of American wheat farms and sugar plantations. In the United States both these crops had relatively short harvest seasons and thus required a relatively brief period of exceptional exertion. But cotton was a different case. The harvest generally began in late August and usually lasted until late December or early January. While one peak of activity was reached in October, daily cotton-picking records indicate that most of the five-month harvest period was marked by a relatively steady level of work. Nor was the harvest season the only or even the most demanding period of pressure on labor. The heaviest demand for labor actually came during the season of cultivation, which extended from mid- or late May through mid- or late July. The planting season, which ran from late March to late April, was still another period of heavy labor demand on cotton plantations.

It was, moreover, misleading to concentrate exclusively on the labor requirements of cotton, since planters chose their secondary crops with the aim of smoothing out the seasonal labor requirements for cotton. Corn was so frequently produced in conjunction with cotton because it could be planted before cotton and harvested either early or late, depending on other pressures. Masters also smoothed the seasonal pattern of labor utilization by scheduling maintenance, new construction, and various indoor tasks during periods when work on crops was slack. As a consequence, such measures as the number of days worked showed little variation from season to season.

The fact that slaves were diligent workers did not have to wait until the 1970s to be discovered. It had been a central finding, decades earlier, of such black historians as Woodson and Charles H. Wesley, who reported the striving of antebellum blacks to acquire skills. These strivings bore fruit, they said, so much so that slaves and free blacks made up over 80 percent of the artisan class of the South. The historians who in the 1970s and 1980s launched new studies of the slave pattern of work, including Cheryll Ann Cody, Douglas Hall, Sidney Mintz, Philip Morgan, Charles Joyner, John Campbell, Daniel C. Littlefield, and Roderick A. McDonald, revived and greatly extended a neglected line of research. One of the new issues investigated in the 1970s and 1980s was the impact of plantation size on the circumstances of the lives of slaves. There was particular interest in the activities of slaves for wages, their role as independent producers of marketable crops and other products, their accomplishments as independent entrepreneurs, and the extent of their provision of credit to fellow slaves—all aspects of the independent slave economy within the plantation regime. In describing the differences in the ways and degrees to which different slaves succeeded in the independent slave economy, scholars also reopened the vexed question of the extent of inequality in the real distribution of the income of slave households.

Cliometricians also contributed to the reconstruction of slave culture by assessing the biases inherent in various bodies of evidence, particularly those sources bearing on the household structure and sexual mores of slaves. Coding, quantifying, and analyzing data from such sources as the probate records of southern courts, the birth and death lists included in the surviving business records of large plantations, and the ex-slave interviews, cliometricians were able to construct distributions of attributes relevant to a number of the points at issue. Crawford, for example, was able to evaluate some of the biases thought to be present in the ex-slave interviews contained in the edition published by Greenwood in 1972. To test the hypothesis that the experience of the Great Depression led ex-slaves to look back favorably on the security of slavery, Crawford compared the responses of slaves interviewed by scholars at Fisk University in 1929 with those interviewed by the WPA in the 1930s and found that the views of the two groups were quite similar.

Crawford also searched for evidence that the responses of ex-slaves were affected by the race of the interviewers. He found suspicious differences in the responses to several questions, but these differences disappeared or became slight when Crawford took into account the characteristics of the ex-slaves who were interviewed by each group. The difference in the characterizations of the diet was a case in point. Among ex-slaves interviewed by blacks, 23.5 percent reported an inadequate diet, but among those interviewed by whites, the proportion reporting inadequate diets was only 14.3 percent—a gap of 9.2 points. When Crawford controlled for plantation size, black interviewers still reported a higher percentage of inadequate diets on large plantations, but the margin of difference between black and white interviewers had declined to 5.5 percent and was no longer statistically significant. Moreover, among ex-slaves from small plantations the relationship ran in the opposite direction, with white interviewers actually reporting a higher percentage of inadequate diets than black interviewers. Crawford concluded that what initially appeared to be an interviewer bias "was largely due to the failure to standardize for the distribution of plantation sizes within the black and white interviewer samples."

More generally, Crawford's statistical analysis of the interviews confirmed the basic assessment of other scholars: taken as a whole, the Greenwood edition represents "an important source of information about slave experiences" but it "does not always replicate the propor-

tions in which various attributes existed in the overall slave population."
He also found that when the investigator paid proper attention to such
matters as the plantation size, the location of the plantation, the principal crop, and the occupation that the ex-slave or his or her parents had
held, it was possible to define subsamples of attributes that were representative of the overall slave population as well as of particular subgroups.

A point that emerges over and over again from Crawford's analysis is
that the size of the plantation was a major determinant of the quality
of slave life. On such matters as the severity of punishment, the supply
of clothing, the occupation of the slave, the stability of the family, and
the uses of leisure time, the experiences of slaves living on small plantations differed significantly from those living on large plantations. Crawford's analysis also suggested that the overrepresentation of large plantations in the sources that particular scholars have favored may have
affected their generalizations about the nature of slave culture. This
point can be illustrated by considering in somewhat greater depth Crawford's findings on the connection between the structure of slave families
and plantation size.

Using the Greenwood sample of interviews, Crawford was able to
construct a distribution of the households in which 742 slaves under
age thirteen were raised. He found that 66 percent lived in two-parent
families, 24 percent in single-parent families (nearly all of which were
headed by mothers), and the rest (about 10 percent) either in the master's house or alone in the quarters. The large percentage of children
raised in two-parent households tends to sustain the belief of Gutman,
Blassingame, and Genovese that the black family emerged from slavery
with a "remarkably stable base." It was, at least, a more stable base than
most slavery scholars had realized before the early 1970s. On the other
hand, one-third of slaves under age thirteen were living in households
from which one or both parents were absent. Crawford's analysis of the
reasons for the large proportion of single-parent households revealed
that in about 60 percent of the cases, the families were broken by the
slave trade or by other features of the slave system. So Frazier appears to
have been correct when he called attention to a dual family structure,

although he underestimated the prevalence of two-parent families and he incorrectly assumed that such families were much more likely to be found among house servants and artisans than among field hands.

Size of plantation was far more important than occupation in determining household structure. Mother-headed families were 50 percent more frequent on plantations with fifteen or fewer slaves than on large ones. These smaller units also had a disproportionately large share of the divided-residence households (families in which the father and mother lived on different plantations for most of the week). Although plantations with fifteen or fewer slaves contained 43 percent of the slave population in 1850, they accounted for nearly two-thirds of all slaves living in divided residences and for over 60 percent of the slaves in one-parent residences. These figures suggest that the conventional family structure was under greater pressure on small units than on large ones. As Crawford points out, on plantations with fifteen or fewer slaves, just one out of three children lived in "fully formed" or conventional households; on plantations of fifty or more slaves, the proportion was reversed.

These proportions pointed out by Crawford help to explain why Gutman found so much more stability and uniformity in the slave family than did Blassingame, Genovese, or Stampp. Gutman's portrait of the slave family was based primarily on his intensive study of the records of six large slaveholdings, located mainly in preponderantly black counties. He chose these particular plantation records because they had exceptional birth registers that permitted him to investigate the marriage patterns of successive generations, to compare the names of children with those of parents and other kin, and to study the evolution of slave families over time.

Records fit to study the intergenerational patterns that so interested Gutman were not likely to be generated on small plantations. All but one of the six plantations in his sample had over one hundred slaves, and the sixth had forty-seven slaves. A sample composed of such large and rapidly growing plantations was quite likely to give much more of an impression of family stability than a representative sample of the entire slave population. Moreover, rapidly growing plantations, because of their exceptional vital rates and age structures, tend to give a misleadingly low impression of the average age of mothers at their first birth. Gutman put the age at about eighteen, which, as James Trussell and Richard H. Steckel pointed out, was biased downward by about three years.

The last point is important because it affected Gutman's generalizations about the sexual mores of adolescent slaves. Assuming that eighteen was the typical age of mothers at first birth and that the average age of menarche (the onset of reproductive capacity) came relatively late for slave women (about sixteen or seventeen), Gutman inferred that slave women generally began their sexual lives at extremely young ages and, unlike white women who were influenced by Victorian values, seldom refrained from having sexual intercourse prior to wedlock. Slave women, he concluded, generally had a child as soon as they were physically capable of having one and not necessarily by the man that they would eventually marry.

Steckel, working with a larger and more representative sample of data, found evidence of significant variation in the sexual practices on plantations of different sizes and in different regions, including evidence that there was more abstention from sexual intercourse among slave women than suggested by Gutman. His data revealed that the proportion of slave women living through their childbearing years without ever bearing a child was higher on large plantations (19 percent) than on small plantations (about 10 percent) and higher on the cotton farms of Georgia and Louisiana (16 percent) than on the tobacco and wheat farms of Virginia (8 percent). Such high rates of childlessness cannot be explained by physiological sterility. For populations as fecund as the U.S. slave population had been, sterility rates are generally less than 5 percent. It thus appears that roughly 10 percent of slave women either largely abstained from sexual intercourse until they reached the end of their childbearing lives or else practiced contraception so effectively that they avoided births throughout these years.

That systematic, sustained practice of contraception was a characteristic of slave society is not sustained by the data in Steckel's samples. His sources showed that the average age of women at the birth of their last child was close to forty. Moreover, for women whose children died within three months of birth, the average interval before the next birth was just nineteen months. Both of these statistics are characteristic of noncontraceptive societies. An analysis of living arrangements also argued against contraception. Steckel's study of plantation registers indicated that few of the women who remained childless throughout the childbearing ages lived with a man. The proportion of couples who were childless was at a level that can be explained by physiological sterility. In other words, infertility was primarily a characteristic of women who did not cohabit with men.

There was also evidence that a large proportion of women who eventually bore children abstained from sexual intercourse for a substantial period after they became fertile. This possibility was suggested by the finding that the average age of women at the birth of their first child was about twenty-one, while the average age of menarche was about 14.5. The relatively early age of puberty implies that if slave women had been having sexual intercourse regularly from menarche on, they would typically have had a child by age sixteen or seventeen. It follows that there was an average interval of adolescent abstention from sexual intercourse lasting at least three years. All told, the sexual mores of slave women appear to have resulted in not making use of roughly one-fifth of their childbearing potential.

Although there remain differences of opinion among cliometricians on various points, and although some traditional historians remain skeptical about some of the cliometric findings, it is now widely agreed that the gang-system plantations were highly profitable and efficient and that the slave economy was thriving on the eve of the Civil War. Moreover, coming to terms with the economic viability of slavery gave a considerable impetus to a reconstruction of the world that the slaves built for themselves and for the remarkable achievements of African Americans under adversity. Slaves were neither lazy nor incompetent. They were energetic and skillful workers, both on their master's account and for themselves. Fathers were not indifferent to their families but sought and found numerous ways to defend and promote family interests under often difficult and threatening circumstances.

Reconsidering the Moral Problem of Slavery

Because new knowledge about the operation of the slave economy contradicted much of the Republican indictment of slavery, Engerman and I grappled with the problem of how to reformulate the moral indictment in a manner that was consistent with the known facts of the actual operation of the slave system. We made a number of suggestions about such a reformulation in *Time on the Cross*. We continued to grapple with the issue during the last half of the 1970s and the 1980s. Enriched by an additional decade and a half of new findings, I decided to make a chapter entitled "The Moral Problem of Slavery" the climax of the final report on our slavery project, which was published in 1989 under the title *Without Consent or Contract*.

In that chapter I argued for a return to the strictly ethical positions taken by the most radical abolitionists in the 1830s, when they still believed that the treatment of southern slaves was mild, and when they considered atrocity stories, some of which they knew were true, to be beside the point. In order to place the radical position within the framework of current imperatives about the content of freedom, I proposed a four-count indictment.

The first, and overarching, count is that slavery gave one group of people the legal right to exercise unrestrained personal domination over another group of people. The proposition that such power was by itself profoundly evil and corrupting was the logical outcome of the theologies of both Quakers and evangelicals. Believing that "all men were equal before God," associating "moral evil with institutions of the external world," holding that it was within the capacity of men to achieve salvation by unselfish acts and unremitting struggle against inward and outward evil, slavery loomed not only as a corrupter of the masters but as a barrier to the exercise of the free will through which slaves could obtain salvation. Personal domination was condemned as a sin, and those who sought it were denounced as usurpers of powers that belonged only to God.

The second count is the denial of economic opportunity. The decisive advantage of the free labor system was not what had been achieved but what was unfolding: the opportunity of the laboring classes to improve their lot as a consequence of rapid technological progress. Unlike the free labor system, there was no mechanism by which slaves could link their incomes to the prosperity of the industries in which they labored.

Denial of citizenship is the third count. Americans slaves were utterly and permanently debarred in every manner possible from a role in law and government. They were deprived not only of the limited common-law rights of the disfranchised European laborers, but even of the few rights enjoyed by slaves in the ecclesiastical courts of Spanish colonies.

Denial of cultural self-identification is the fourth count in the new indictment. It might seem odd to include this point as a major count when many slavery historians emphasize the cultural autonomy of slaves. Yet it would be unfortunate and misleading if current research aimed at defining slave culture and at revealing the role of slaves in shaping that culture served to mitigate the condemnation of southern and West Indian masters for their ceaseless attempts to achieve cultural domination. One of the most important points that has emerged from the work of cultural historians is the intimate connection between political power and culture. The explosive growth of black churches, businesses, political clubs, and fraternal organizations after the Civil War mirrored working-class experiences in Europe and underscores the immense importance of freedom (even the "half" freedom of a thwarted Reconstruction) for the development of black cultural self-identification.

There is still the ominous paradox that gang labor was more efficient than free labor. That paradox is only apparent. It collapses under scrutiny, not because the new economic findings are false, but because the paradox rests on the widely held assumption that technological efficiency is inherently good. It is this beguiling assumption that is false and, when applied to slavery, insidious. In and of itself, economic or technological efficiency is neither moral nor immoral. The virtue of an efficient technique depends exclusively on its moral nature or the moral purposes that it serves. One need not be an evangelical Protestant or a pious believer of any other formal religion to agree that moral values, rather than economic, political, or scientific achievements, are the supreme guides for human behavior. When we celebrate such technological advances as the blast furnace, electricity, and medical surgery, it is not because they are intrinsically good but because they have usually served well the great ethical goals of humankind. Nevertheless, each of these innovations has been used at various times for demonic ends. Slavery was a somewhat different case. It was intrinsically evil because its productive efficiency arose directly out of the oppression of its laborers. The efficiency of slavery seemed paradoxical not because an intrinsically good or a morally neutral technology was made to serve an evil purpose, but because an intrinsically evil technology was so productive. Discarding the assumption that productivity is necessarily virtuous resolves the paradox.

The work of the cliometricians also reshaped the moral problem of slavery by undermining the proposition that slavery would have died of its own economic contradictions, a proposition that was welcomed by the generation of historians disillusioned by the outcome of World War I. The idea that slavery was doomed by its tendency toward the overproduction of cotton not only seemed reasonable during and after the Depression decade of the 1930s, but it was comforting to those historians who wished to be free of the agonizing choice between the sin of war and the sin of slavery. In light of cliometric findings, it now appears that the thriving economic system of the slaveholding South would not have been destroyed without a war or at least a powerful military threat from a coalition of countries. That is the conclusion that William Lloyd Garrison reached when he abandoned his pacifism and endorsed the Union cause.

However, the political, and ultimately military, defeat of slavery was not foreordained. It was extremely difficult to build a coalition that could wrest control from the plantation magnates whose enormous wealth and political skills had enabled them to control the federal government for more than half a century. Indeed, among those who were instrumental in creating the Republican party, differences of opinion over the feasibility of building a winning coalition on a purely sectional basis extended over nearly a decade. Only devout abolitionists such as

Joshua R. Giddings and Salmon P. Chase considered it a serious option in 1848. Horace Greeley did not reach that conclusion for another six years. William H. Seward and Thurlow Weed lagged behind Greeley by a year and a half, and Lincoln was still unsure at the start of 1856. These doubts were not without foundation. There were numerous contingent circumstances that had to yield fortunate outcomes in order to bring a purely northern coalition to power.

TOWARD A NEW SYNTHESIS ON THE SHAPING OF
AMERICAN CIVILIZATION

Once it became clear that the slave economy was thriving on the eve of
the Civil War, the debates over how the slave system actually worked
naturally spilled over to the issue of how the slave system was brought
down. Few of the slavery specialists and almost none of the cliometricians had previously worked on the political history of the antebellum
era. The political crises of the North and their social and economic
causes originally seemed remote from the issues defined by Phillips and
Stampp. In this lecture I want to describe how these two streams of research—slavery studies and political history—became closely inter-
twined and how together they have contributed to an emerging new
synthesis on the shaping of American civilization. The story begins with
the revolt against progressive history.

Challenging the Progressive Synthesis

At about the same time that Stampp launched his attack on the
Phillips school, a new generation of intellectual and political historians
began to undermine the progressive synthesis that dominated American historiography between the end of World War I and the early 1950s.
Shaped by three inventive and powerful writers of history, the progressive tradition exhibited the same kind of robustness that characterized
the scholarly output of Phillips, who was also part of the progressive
tradition.

Born during the 1860s and 1870s, the three leading progressive historians were by and large rebels against the strict religiosity of their
childhood. They embraced science, Darwinism, the higher criticism,
and the progressive agenda of social and economic reform. But they did
not welcome the relentless advance of modern commerce and industry, and they viewed the huge cities of the early twentieth century as
dire threats to the way of life that they identified with the midwestern
towns in which they were raised. Frederick Jackson Turner, Charles

Beard, and Vernon Lewis Parrington were convinced that economic factors were the driving force of American history. Turner was more willing than Beard or Parrington to recognize that slavery was a factor in precipitating the Civil War. Yet he saw slavery as only one of many factors arising from geographic differences and economic conflicts, not just between the North and the South, but also between each of those two sections and the West.

Beard, on the other hand, subordinated all other issues to the struggle between rival economic systems for political control of the nation, excluding the ethics of slavery as a fundamental issue. The Civil War was a revolution that made it possible for the industrial capitalists of the Northeast (in alliance with the free farmers of the Midwest) to wrest political control from the planter class, thus ending the agricultural era of American history. Yet Beard was alarmed by the outcome of the revolution, which produced a bloated industrial-commercial plutocracy, a huge army of impoverished wage workers, and periodic outbreaks of bitter class warfare. Parrington reinforced Beard's economic interpretation, as he also saw a three-region economic conflict. Although the war eliminated slavery, it led to national domination by eastern capitalism, which strangled the agrarian democracy of the West and imposed what Parrington called "a universal cash-register evaluation of life."

The challenge to the hold of the progressives on the interpretation of American civilization began in a corner of American historiography that was far from the mainstream of political history. The challenge arose from a new generation of historians of religion who increasingly approached their subject matter as a subfield of intellectual history and became imbued with the sociological approach to the study of religion. During the 1950s and 1960s a series of books focusing not on abolitionism but on the transformation of the evangelical churches during the Second Great Awakening indirectly called attention to the central role of the evangelical churches in fashioning an antislavery ethic and political movement. One of the earliest and most influential of these studies was *The Burned-Over District: The Social and Intellectual History of En-*

thusiastic Religion in Western New York, 1800–1850, by Whitney R. Cross, which showed how the perfectionist, millennialist aspects of the revival spawned a series of single-issue organizations that sought to reform America. The causes espoused by these organizations ranged from the promotion of Sunday schools and the strict observance of the Sabbath to temperance, pacifism, anti-Catholicism and nativism, health reform, the abolition of slavery, and the rights of aboriginal peoples. Cross and other religious historians also spelled out the evolution of these movements from exhortation to political mobilizations aimed at legislative reform to direct participation in politics.

In the course of laying bare the social forces that promoted change in American theology and religious institutions, these historians sketched the development of a distinct "Yankee Culture" rooted in Puritanism, which had evolved into a "New Divinity." They also chronicled the social and economic transformation of New England between 1630 and 1850, which included the exodus of hundreds of thousands of New Englanders into a Yankee diaspora that extended to the Missouri River and lay mainly above the 40th parallel. Favored by unusually low mortality rates and high fertility rates, the descendants of the Puritans became so numerous that by 1820 they accounted for the great bulk of the northern population. A parallel history of the development of evangelical religion emerged for the South, which helped to define distinctive aspects of southern culture.

These developments in religious history helped to precipitate two new schools of political history, which came to be known as the "ethnocultural school" and the historians of political culture. Lee Benson's *The Concept of Jacksonian Democracy,* published in 1961, launched the ethnocultural approach, challenging the progressive tradition, which made class conflict the principal source of political divisions. Benson argued that during the Jacksonian era, and particularly in the election of 1844, ethnic and religious conflicts were far more decisive than class conflicts, with Catholic voters strongly supporting the Democrats and evangelical Protestants strongly supporting the Whigs. Although Benson's evidence on voting behavior was quite limited, later studies in the ethnocultural tradition marshaled support for the thesis in studies of several northern states before the Civil War and in midwestern voting patterns generally between 1850 and 1892.

Historians of political culture treated the various political parties as distinct cultures defined by their programs, ideologies, constituencies, and leaders. One of the earliest of these works, by Marvin Meyers, sought to define the culture of the Democratic party under Jackson. Subsequent studies have brought cultural analysis to bear on the Whigs, the Federalists, the Democrats during the middle decades of the nineteenth century, the early Republican party, and the Antimasonic and Know-Nothing parties. One of the most influential of these studies was Eric Foner's *Free Soil, Free Labor, Free Men: The Ideology of the Republican Party before the Civil War.* The two decades preceding the war, said Foner, "witnessed the development of conflicting sectional ideologies, each viewing its own society as fundamentally well-ordered, and the other as both a negation of its most cherished values and a threat to its existence." When the Republican party came into being, it sought to mobilize its forces around the proposition that "two profoundly different and antagonistic civilizations were competing for control of the political system." The debate touched off by Foner's book helped to push research toward a more complex and more directly political analysis of the breakup of the second party system and of the political realignment of the 1850s.

Cultural historians of the South, such as Eugene Genovese, have focused more on the evolving culture of the planter class and of southern yeomen than on the particular cultural dimensions that distinguished the parties of the South. In this work, attitudes toward religion—including the strong anticlerical strain among some leading figures in the planter class, the influence of a cult of honor (among other premodern values), and the elevation in southern theology of the inner struggles against sin over the New Divinity's focus on the ethic of benevolence—were heavily emphasized.

Still another factor favoring the integration of cultural and political history was the emergence of a new history of the antislavery movement covering developments on both sides of the Atlantic. This literature sought to weave the religious, social, economic, political, and cultural trends in America and Great Britain into a description of the worldwide movement that successfully destroyed slavery, in order to explain how a thriving economic system that had stood above criticism for three thousand years was outlawed everywhere in the Western World only a century after the political onslaught was launched.

This new work burst upon the scene in the 1960s and corralled an impressive proportion of major prizes for historical literature. Its first classic, *The Problem of Slavery in Western Culture* by David Brion Davis, won the Pulitzer Prize in history in 1967, and Davis's 1975 volume, *The Problem of Slavery in the Age of Revolution,* won the National Book Award. In 1969 Winthrop D. Jordan won the National Book Award for *White over Black,* which, like Davis's first volume, traced the evolution of ideologies justifying black slavery and the rise of early abolitionist ideology. The literature in this field is too large to be described adequately here, but other key contributions are Roger Anstey's *The Atlantic Slave Trade and British Abolition, 1760–1810* (1975); two volumes by Seymour Drescher: *Econocide: British Slavery in the Era of Abolition* (1977) and *Capitalism and Antislavery* (1986); Richard H. Sewell's *Ballots for Freedom: Antislavery Politics in the United States, 1837–1860* (1976); Howard Temperley's *British Antislavery, 1833–1970* (1972); and M. I. Finley's *Ancient Slavery and Modern Ideology* (1980).

The "new" political history—the statistical analysis of voting behavior in Congress or other legislatures and the popular sources of electoral support—is still another ingredient of the postprogressive approach to political history. Gutman scaling has been used to identify the legislative issues that defined the differences between Whigs and Democrats and between Radical Republicans and other Republicans and to explain the breakup of coalitions as issues shifted. Roll-call analysis has been used to show how geographic expansion destabilized the second party system and turned slavery into a realigning issue. Ecological regressions have been used to identify the religious, economic, and ethnic bases for the popular support of parties in particular elections and for shifts in such support over time. Simulation models have been employed to show how changes in the ethnic and religious composition of the electorate and shifts of ethnoreligious groups from the Democrats to the Republicans contributed to the political realignment of the 1850s.

Since the weaving of these various strands of research into a new interpretation of the political realignment of the 1850s is still in progress, the end of the odyssey cannot yet be described. But some elements of the emerging consensus can be sketched. It is clear that slavery became the paramount ethical issue of the radical northern evangelicals and that they succeeded to a large extent in convincing northerners that the planter class of the South (and their political accomplices, North and South) were not only corrupt but a menace to the spiritual salvation of the North. It is also clear that the widespread acceptance of this proposition by northern Whigs split the party along sectional lines in the early 1850s. Another point of consensus is on the destabilizing impact of overrapid urban growth in the North and of the huge influx of Catholic and Lutheran immigrants (mainly from Ireland and Germany), which greatly changed the character of the northern electorate in a way that was extremely threatening to "Old Americans" (third-or-greater-generation Americans who were mainly evangelicals of British stock or pietistic Germans). This fear gave rise to the Know-Nothings, a nativist political movement that attracted large numbers of Old Americans from both the Whig and Democratic parties in the North.

Antislavery leaders in conjunction with dissident Whigs and Democrats adroitly exploited this period of political flux to create a new coalition, called the Republican party, which made opposition to slavery (southern) expansion into the North its key plank, but which also had strong nativist and anti-Catholic overtones. The key aspect of this realignment was the flight of Old Americans in the North from the Democratic party (which was seen as pandering to the "New Americans"). In 1852 over 48 percent of northern Old Americans voted Democratic, and they accounted for 63 percent of the Democratic vote in the North; but in 1860 barely 30 percent of Old Americans voted Democratic, and they accounted for less than 40 percent of the northern Democratic vote. It was the consolidation of Old Americans in the Republican party on an antislavery, antisouthern, and anti-Catholic program that gave the coalition its margin of victory.

The replacement of the progressive synthesis made it possible to reconsider the role of economic issues in the political realignment. Economic analysis was no longer burdened by the vision of two incompatible economic systems locked in a titanic struggle that only one system could survive. Five decades of economic research revealed that the economies of both the North and South experienced vigorous long-term economic growth spurred by rapid technological change. Both regions also experienced periodic economic crises that brought financial instability and often severe unemployment among artisans and low-skilled laborers, pitting native and foreign-born workers against each other.

Far from being incompatible, the economies of the two regions were closely tied to each other by intricate webs of trade and commerce. The South was a prime market for the products of the North's rapidly expanding manufacturing sector, especially textiles, shoes, iron, and steel. Indeed, mass-produced clothing for slaves accounted for a significant share of the output of northern textile mills. Among the products that the South supplied to the North were raw cotton, tobacco, refined sugar, and molasses. Both regions experienced a two-way flow of capital and commercial services. Southern planters invested in railroads north of the Mason-Dixon Line, and northern capital helped to finance southern commerce and plantations. Most of the businessmen of each region saw the businesses of the other regions less as threats to their own interests than as partners in advancing a common prosperity. When antislavery militants sought to promote political coalitions hostile to the South, many northern merchants and factory owners counseled compromise.

Economic Issues in the Political Realignment of the 1850s

Although economic issues played an important part in the political realignment of the 1850s, there was no one persistent issue that by itself can explain that realignment. Nor were economic issues more dominant than ideological, political, social, or cultural issues. Like other issues, economic issues waxed and waned, and as they did, politicians sought to exploit each in turn to advance their political objectives. Among these politicians were a small number who were dedicated to the abolition of slavery and who were able to exploit the breakdown of the second party system to advance their objectives. During the early decades of the industrial revolution, when many economic and social issues were in flux, competing groups of politicians were struggling to find ways of turning the often novel issues to their advantage. It was the political retailing of a changing basket of economic issues, not a continuous and increasingly deadly struggle between antithetical economic systems, that characterized the politics of the 1840s and the 1850s. Within that framework, several different ways in which economic issues flowed into and out of northern politics can be discerned.

First, there were the early, initially unsuccessful efforts by abolitionists to insert an economic dimension into the abolitionist indictments of the South by charging that southerners were draining northern capital by borrowing heavily from northen merchants and banks. This period of early experimentation with economic issues extended from the late 1830s to the late 1840s.

There was also the rise of a new set of economic issues, quite different from those that originally defined the second party system, which were related to the explosive rate of urbanization and the unprecedented rate of immigration. These issues arose sporadically between 1820 and 1844 and came to the fore between 1848 and 1855. The acute phase of political reaction reflected a triple economic crisis (declining real wages, rising unemployment, and deteriorating health and life expectancy) experienced by northern nonfarm workers. Concern about unchecked immigration and the attendant crises was critical to the spontaneous breakaway of nativist workers in the North from the Whig and Democratic parties during the years 1851–55.

A third phase in the development of economic issues began when certain antislavery leaders sought to exploit the Kansas crisis in order to gain control of the nativist breakaway and push it in an antislavery direction. Not all of the antislavery leaders in the Whig, Democratic, and Free Soil parties appreciated the need to stress the economic dimension, but Henry Wilson and Joshuà R. Giddings (who were originally Whigs), Galusha A. Grow and Nathaniel P. Banks (who were originally Democrats), and especially Horace Greeley did.

The next aspect of the development of economic issues involved the effort to consolidate and extend Republican support between the end of the 1856 election and the outbreak of the crisis of 1857. During this period of economic recovery in the North, Republican leaders led by Greeley intensified the economic indictment of the South, exploiting the antislavery books by Frederick Law Olmsted and (especially) Hinton Rowan Helper, and arguing that the expansionist impulse of the South stemmed from its economic failure.

Another phase in the development of economic issues occurred after the outbreak of the crisis of 1857, which strained Republican unity. Republicans were let off the hook, however, by the brevity of the crisis and the strong recovery, as well as by the outrage of the Democrats over Helper's book, which became the center of the struggle to organize the House in December 1859 and January 1860.

Finally, the attempt to promote economic issues took a new turn when Buchanan vetoed the Homestead Bill, which sought to provide federal lands free to settlers in the West, in June 1860. This was the culmination of a process that turned the demand for free land from a divisive issue in Republican ranks into a unifying issue.

In analyzing the economic component of the political realignment of the 1850s, it is important to keep in mind that the economic issues just summarized were not part of some underlying general economic crisis of capitalism. From the standpoint of economics, they are relatively distinct issues whose coherence was mostly a product of political rhetoric. I stress this point because not enough attention has been given to the disjunctions in economic developments across regions and classes during the antebellum era. On this issue, some cliometricians have been among the worst sinners.

In *Without Consent or Contract* I referred to the economic distress that afflicted native northern nonfarm workers during the 1850s as a "hidden depression" because of the scant attention it had received from cliometricians up to that point. The main emphasis of cliometric research, including my own, during the 1960s and 1970s was on measuring long-term trends in economic growth. We tended to neglect short-term business cycles as brief phenomena superimposed on such a strong upward secular pattern of growth in per capita income and real wages that they did not undermine the view that the period from 1840 to 1860 was one of general prosperity. We were aware that labor historians had a much dimmer view of the period, emphasizing the hardships experienced by the urban laboring classes, but their evidence was mainly anecdotal and easy to dismiss.

As it turned out, the anecdotal evidence was more revealing of year-to-year conditions of life than our reliance on estimates of per capita income in census years. That conclusion was forced upon us in the 1980s when cliometricians began collecting evidence on year-to-year changes in mortality rates and final heights (a sensitive indicator of general health during developmental ages). These measures revealed severe declines in longevity and rapid deterioration in health, despite the substantial increase in per capita income from one census year to another, with the worst problems in the large northern cities. Consequently, cliometricians, especially those concerned with the impact of economic conditions on political alignments, had to return to the study of business cycles. More recently, cliometricians such as Robert Margo have undertaken the study of cyclical trends in wages and employment during the nineteenth century.

Of the seven business cycles between the end of the War of 1812 and the outbreak of the Civil War, only those of 1819–20 and 1837–38 were similar in their regional impact. The northern recession of 1826–28 was a depression in the South that lasted until 1831. Similarly, the brief though sharp northern recession of 1841–43 began in the South a year earlier, lasted two years longer, and was more severe. On the other hand, the severe northern recession of 1857–58 coincided with one of the South's most vigorous booms. The impact of immigrants on labor markets, so devastating to native artisans in the North during the first half of the 1850s, was much more confined in the South.

The way in which the railroad-building boom unfolded also did more to destabilize the economy of the Northwest than of the South during the 1850s. Although the South and the Northwest showed a similar pattern of rising construction between 1849 and 1853, construction dropped off sharply in the Northwest after 1853. The rate of decline in that region was so rapid that by 1859 the annual rate of construction was not only far below its 1853 peak, it was even below the level that had prevailed at the beginning of the decade. In the South, annual railroad construction fell off only in 1854 and 1855. It rose sharply in each of the remaining years of the decade. By 1859, southern construction was not only three times greater than it had been at the start of the 1850s, it was also well above the 1853 peak.

The disjunctions in economic experience across classes of free workers are most visible in the North, where a spontaneous political protest movement of nativist workers arose during a period of generally strong economic growth. It is unlikely that the nativist political movement would have come close to the northern successes it obtained in 1853–55 without the pressures on labor markets generated by the massive immigration of 1848–54, by the high inflation rates of those years, by the massive dumping of immigrant railroad workers onto the labor markets of the states of the Old Northwest beginning about 1853, and by the acute public health crisis of 1849–55 (promoted by a combination of massive immigration and overrapid urban expansion), during which cholera and other alarming diseases became endemic in the major cities of the North.

These economic issues arose quite independently of the antislavery movement and were entirely outside of the realm of economic issues originally raised by the antislavery militants. It was not until the Kansas crisis that a handful of antislavery militants saw a method of developing economic issues in such a way that they would not only make deep inroads into the growing Know-Nothing constituency but would also appeal to the northern left-wing, class-oriented militants of the Democratic party, many of whom had seized on the free land issue as a panacea. Democrats of this stripe were appalled when passage of the Kansas-Nebraska Act in the spring of 1854 was coupled with the defeat of the Homestead Bill as Democrats in the South Atlantic states, fearful of the political implications of the massive immigration into the

North, reversed their position and voted against land reform as a bloc. Labor leaders who had been aloof from the antislavery movement suddenly began to accept the theory that there really was a "slave power" conspiracy aimed not merely at thwarting their campaign for a homestead act but at bringing slaves into direct competition with free northern labor.

Horace Greeley was far more prescient than other Whig leaders in recognizing the potential for merging the free land and free soil questions by hooking them onto the Kansas issue. He was more than a year ahead of Thurlow Weed and William Seward, and close to two years ahead of Lincoln, in concluding that this combination of issues provided the opportunity to create a winning coalition, one comprising primarily northern Whigs but with the potential for drawing in key elements of the left-labor Democrats and luring back northern Whigs who had bolted to the Know-Nothings. Of course, Weed, as a coalition builder, faced constraints that required him to proceed more deliberately and cautiously than an issue innovator. Greeley may have been capricious in personal and political relationships and lacking in the patience and steadiness needed to forge a broad leadership for the new coalition, but he was superb in charting and promoting a new ideological line.

It is true that economic issues were not at the center of the Republican appeal in 1856. They certainly were not put into the 1856 platform. But nativist issues that played an important role in the Republican campaign were also omitted from the platform. There were good reasons for such reticence. Although both anti-Catholicism and nativism appealed to major sections of the Republican constituency, they were too divisive to be the basis for a coalition consensus. So the anti-Catholic and nativist appeals were left to those newspapers and organizations within the Republican coalition that wished to promote them. Given the fragility of the Republican coalition, the official program had to be confined to those points that united the subgroups of the party.

Thus, while all components of the coalition pushed the antislavery theme, there was an understandable rhetorical division of labor among the elements of the coalition, each element combining the central antislavery theme with those subthemes most congenial to its particular constituencies. In 1855 and 1856, Massachusetts Republicans such as Nathaniel P. Banks and Henry Wilson combined antislavery with labor and nativist appeals, whereas Greeley tried to counter the nativist appeal (until 1856) and worked assiduously to give an economic dimension to the antislavery appeal, which he aimed especially at journeymen and farmers. These Republican strategists recognized that to counter the nativist appeal effectively, there had to be at least a rhetorical identification with the economic concerns of the Know-Nothing constituency. Robert C. Winthrop gave recognition to the role of economic issues in the Republican campaign of 1856, which he described as one-third Missouri Compromise, one-third Kansas outrages, and "one-third disjointed and misapplied figures, and a great swelling of words and vanity, to prove that the South is, upon the whole, the very poorest, meanest, least productive, and most miserable part of creation."

Between early 1856 and late 1857, economic issues played a different role than they had from 1851 to 1855. The economic recovery of the North between 1855 and mid-1857, the relatively steady price level, and the sharp reduction in immigration sapped the vitality of the Know Nothing movement (which focused on economic problems in the North) and permitted Republicans to push the theme of the superiority of the northern economy over the southern economy. During this period, Greeley reinvigorated the economic indictment of slavery, seizing upon Helper's book, which he enthusiastically promoted in the New York *Tribune* with an initial eight-column story and follow-ups.

The economic crisis of 1857–58 posed a severe threat to the Republican coalition, not only because it was almost exclusively a northern crisis, but also because the various elements of the coalition differed on policies to alleviate the crisis. The coalition was spared a split on this issue by several fortunate events: the swift, sharp recovery that began in 1858; the continuing drop in immigration, which eased pressures on labor markets; and the decline in food prices, which served to raise the real wages of workers in both urban and rural areas. These conditions made it possible for Republicans in 1859 and 1860 to press their theme that the booming northern economy was infinitely superior to that of the South and that northern prosperity was endangered by an economically backward slave South that saw expansion into the North as the only solution to its otherwise hopeless economic bankruptcy. Southern leaders, made exceedingly self-confident and increasingly nationalistic by the powerful economic boom in the South that occupied most of the decade, took the northern bait. Their outrage over the northern calumny of their economic and social system turned attention away from northern economic problems (which were only temporarily alleviated) and gave credence to the claim that the North was menaced by the political and economic aggression of the South.

The use of the land-reform issue also changed from 1854–55 to 1859–60. During the first period, although a divisive issue in Republican ranks, land reform contributed to the defection of some militant labor leaders from the Democratic party. It also helped to infuse the "slave power" slogan with economic content. By 1859–60, after southern hostility to a homestead act became overwhelming, and especially after Buchanan announced his intention to veto the pending bill (a threat he carried out in June 1860), land reform became a unifying issue in Republican ranks. So the Republican platform of 1860 combined the two slogans—keeping the territories for free men and land reform—in much the same way that they had been combined by the left-labor forces of 1854.

Dissecting the Myth of an Impoverished South

Did the struggle against slavery decisively reshape American civilization? The weight of evidence brought to light during the slavery debates clearly indicates that it did, but not because it rescued an impoverished, economically stagnating region from the clutches of an economically bankrupt planter class. Cliometric research has revealed that the planter class was thriving during the last two decades of the antebellum era and was every bit as prosperous as the rich of the North, although the source of the wealth of the two plutocracies differed. The North's wealthiest 1 percent in 1860 were mainly urban merchants and manufacturers whose businesses were based on wage labor, while in the South the top 1 percent were mainly rural planters whose businesses were based on slave labor. The southern plutocrats were considerably richer on average than their northern counterparts, by a factor of roughly two to one. Indeed, nearly two out of every three males in the United States with wealth of $100,000 or more (the super rich of the era) lived in the South in 1860.

The big planters of the cotton belt were generally consolidating their economic positions during the late antebellum era. Between 1850 and 1860 the real wealth of the typical gang-system planter increased by 70 percent. Rather than gradually slipping from its economic dominance, this class was overthrown by the Civil War, which led to the destruction or loss of two-thirds of its wealth. By 1870 southerners no longer predominated among the nation's super rich; four out of every five of the super rich were now northerners. So it was not the vagaries of the market or other economic events but military defeat that moved the scepter of wealth from the agrarian South to the industrializing North.

If we treat the North and South as separate nations and rank them among the countries of the world, the South would stand as the fourth most prosperous nation of the world in 1860. The South was more prosperous than France, Germany, Denmark, or any of the countries of Europe except England. The South was not only advanced by antebellum standards but also by relatively recent standards. Indeed, a country as advanced as Italy did not achieve the southern level of per capita income until the eve of World War II.

The last point underscores the dubious nature of attempts to classify the South as a "colonial dependency." The South's large purchases of manufactured goods from the North made it no more of a colonial dependency than did the North's heavy purchases of rails from Great Britain. The true colonial dependencies, countries such as India and Mexico, had less than one-tenth the per capita income of the South in 1860.

Much of the antislavery ammunition for the characterization of the South as a land of poverty was drawn from the debates on economic policy among southern leaders, especially during the economic crisis of the 1840s and during the political crises of the 1850s. As sectional tensions mounted, southerners became increasingly alarmed by federal policies that they thought were giving economic advantage to the North. They also became increasingly impatient with what they thought was an insufficiently active role by the their state and local governments to promote internal improvements and to embrace other policies that would accelerate the southern rate of economic growth. To generate a sense of urgency, and to develop a spirit of unity against pro-northern economic policies, southern newspapers, journals, economic leaders, and politicians continually emphasized every unrealized objective of the South. The regionwide economic conventions that were regularly organized to promote southern interests took on an increasingly nationalistic character, with "radical" politicians using economic arguments to promote support for a secessionist policy. By the mid-1850s southern discussions of economic issues were, if not the handmaiden of nationalistic politics, deeply entangled in it.

Far from stagnating, the per capita income of the South grew at an average annual rate of 1.7 percent from 1840 to 1860. This rate of growth was not only a third higher than that enjoyed by the North but quite high by historical standards. Only a handful of countries have been able to sustain long-term growth rates substantially in excess of that achieved by the antebellum South between 1840 and 1860.

The charge that the South was irrationally addicted to overproduction of cotton and other staples did not disappear with the Civil War but remained a point of contention during the postbellum era. Some reformers attributed the depressed state of the southern economy between 1865 and 1880 and beyond to the failure of southern farmers to diversify their crops. Some attributed the rigidity to a hangover of bad habits developed during the antebellum era, and some emphasized the lack of experience of blacks in crops other than cotton. Others put the blame on merchants and landlords who forced tenants to grow excessive cotton so that the tenants would have to buy food and other supplies from their stores at excessively high prices and (if purchased on credit) at usurious rates of interest. But perhaps the most common explanation for the overproduction of cotton was a presumed addiction to cash crops and an overemphasis on short-run profits. Reformers accused southern farmers of failing to appreciate the benefits of being self-sufficient because self-sufficiency often meant a lowered average income. Critics who made these points often acknowledged that in good times concentration on cotton brought the highest profit but stressed that such a policy not only left farmers extremely vulnerable when cotton prices were low but bred the vain hope that prices "would rally again." "Multitudes of men" harbored this delusion "year after year" and "seemed utterly unable to tear themselves away from its constantly fastening power."

Cliometricians have been able to test empirically the proposition that planters were irrationally attached to cotton production and unresponsive to price signals and profits. They have estimated the speed with which southern farmers changed the mix of crops in response to a change in the relative prices of these crops. Farmers in all regions of the United States as well as in other countries respond to changing prices with a lag; that is, they do not switch entirely into or out of a given crop in one year just because the price in the previous year was higher or lower than they expected it to be. Instead, farmers usually make only a partial adjustment in a single year, waiting for further evidence as to whether a previous change in price was just a chance fluctuation or a lasting change. A common measure of the responsiveness of farmers, then, is the number of years it takes for them to make a 90 percent adjustment to a lasting change in prices. It has now been shown that southern farmers in the postbellum era were just as responsive to lasting price changes as the wheat farmers in the North. In both instances farmers made a 90 percent adjustment in about five years.

What about the slave era? The speed of adjustment was more rapid before the Civil War than after it. Slave owners made a 90 percent adjustment in their output of cotton within just two years after a lasting price change. Far from lagging behind nonslaveholding farmers in responding to price changes, the big cotton planters appear to have responded with uncommon speed, perhaps because, as one cliometrician has suggested, their stronger financial position permitted them to take greater risks than a small farmer was willing to incur. In hindsight, this tendency does not seem surprising. After all, the speed with which slave-holders reacted to the sudden change in the price of indigo after the Revolution came demonstrates their sensitivity to market conditions. In that instance, slaveholders reduced their slave-produced crop by 98 percent in just three years, and they never returned to indigo again because the price of that crop never warranted a return.

What about the contention that the surge in cotton production during the 1850s, especially the leap in production between 1857 and 1860, was symptomatic of a long-term tendency toward the overproduction of cotton? There was nothing so unusual about the rate or manner in which cotton production increased during the 1850s that warrants such a conclusion. Similar booms were experienced during every decade of the nineteenth century except for the depression decade of the 1840s. Indeed, the annual rate of increase in cotton production between 1857 and 1860 was actually a bit below the average rate during other years in which cotton production increased. Nor was it particularly unusual for output to have increased for three years in a row. There were four other long expansions between 1806 and 1860, one of which lasted ten years.

Those who advocated the overproduction thesis did not treat the 1857–60 expansion as a fifth major cotton boom because of the slight decline in the price of cotton that occurred during these years. But there were comparable declines in the price of cotton during the booms of the second, third, and fourth decades of the nineteenth century. Moreover, the general trend of raw cotton prices was downward from 1802 on. Although there were fluctuations in this trend, the average annual rate of decrease was 0.7 percent. The basic cause of this long-term decline was the steady increase in productivity. Among the developments that made cotton farming increasingly more efficient were improvements in the varieties of cottonseeds, introduction of the cotton gin, reduction in transportation and other marketing costs, and relocation of cotton production to the more fertile lands of the New South.

It was therefore to be expected that increases in production would generally be associated with declining prices. Since advances in productivity caused costs to fall, profits of planters may have been rising despite declining cotton prices. What is crucial, then, is not the absolute level of prices but the level of profits. An approximation of the movement of profits may be obtained by examining the deviation of cotton prices from their long-term trend. When cotton prices were above their long-term trend value, profits of planters were likely to have been above normal. When prices were below their trend values, profits on cotton were likely to have been below normal.

Cliometricians have shown that the 1850s thus constituted a period of sustained boom in profits for cotton planters. Nearly every year of the decade was one of above-normal profit. What is more, profits remained high during the last four years of the decade, with prices averaging about 15 percent above their trend values. No wonder cotton production doubled between 1850 and 1860. It was clearly a rational economic response to increase cotton production by more than 50 percent between 1857 and 1860. If planters erred, it was not in expanding cotton production too much but in being too conservative. Their expansion had not been adequate to bring prices down to their trend values and profits back to normal (equilibrium) levels.

What was responsible for making the 1850s so prosperous for cotton planters? One answer is that the worldwide demand for southern cotton began to increase rapidly beginning in 1846. During most of the 1850s the supply of cotton lagged behind the demand, which caused the price of cotton to rise well above normal levels, creating unusually large profits for planters. While planters responded to this incentive, they did not increase output rapidly enough to return cotton prices and profits to a normal level by 1860.

Perhaps the most important, and the most neglected, aspect of cliometric findings about the antebellum economy is that during the years between 1840 and 1860, when the South was growing more rapidly than the North, it was not primarily developments within the agricultural sector that explained the South's favorable performance. The main factor was the restructuring of the southern economy, which involved a substantial shift of resources from agriculture to the nonagricultural sectors. It was political, not economic, forces that checked this restructuring. The Civil War devastated the southern economy, with per capita output in 1870 reduced to two-thirds of the 1860 level.

How the Antislavery Struggle Reshaped American Civilization

Some historians argue that nobody seriously believed or believes that economic efficiency is in and of itself good. Yet the belief that virtue and economic progress are interconnected is deep in American culture, and it was a particularly prominent aspect of the antislavery struggle. The tenacity with which abolitionists clung to the contention that emancipation was bringing prosperity in the West Indies, despite all the contrary evidence, strongly suggests that they were swayed by a theory that told them that their expectation of prosperity had to be correct, a theory to which they were so deeply committed that their theoretical knowledge swept aside all empirical evidence to the contrary. There was, of course, such a theory, or more appropriately, a theological proposition, in the evangelical creed. That was the proposition that divine providence rewarded virtue and punished evil. The proposition continues to be widely accepted today not only among Protestant evangelicals but also among individuals with highly secular philosophies. The secular version is embodied in a nontheistic optimism that "events" reward virtue and punish evil. Whether theological or secular in origin this optimistic theory implies that immoral economic systems cannot be productive, for that would reward evil, and moral systems cannot be unproductive, for that would punish virtue. The theory operates in two directions. If something is known to be evil, it cannot work well (slavery must have been inefficient; capitalism is bound to die of its internal economic contradictions; totalitarian societies must be less productive than democratic societies). Alternatively, systems that fail must be evil (the French Revolution proves that the *ancien régime* was economically corrupt; the overthrow of slave systems proves their economic backwardness; the incidents at Three Mile Island and at Chernobyl prove not only the danger but the immorality of nuclear energy programs).

The antislavery struggle reshaped American civilization by incorporating the ethics of radical northern evangelicals and Quakers into the secular creed of the American state. The proposition that unrestrained personal domination of one group of people over another is profoundly evil, once a highly factious religious viewpoint, is now so deeply embedded in modern democratic thought that virtually every organized political force in American life accepts it, often without realizing its religious origin. The antislavery struggle also secularized the ethics of benevolence, ultimately laying the basis for the welfare state and for the use of fiscal power to redistribute income and wealth from the rich to the poor.

The antislavery struggle also demonstrated that populist political movements could turn the federal government into a powerful instrument for implementing their reform programs. In so doing they developed constitutional justifications and tactics for mobilizing popular support that have been copied and amplified by reform movements down to the present day. These successes contributed heavily to the changing balance of power between the federal government and state and local governments, and also to the changing balance of power between employers and employees. A more subtle but still powerful consequence of the antislavery struggle was the creation of a permanent cadre of reformers prepared to champion the interests of the underprivileged. This cadre has been renewed generation after generation, creating a genealogy of reformers that is still intact.

The progressive historians believed in a tighter connection between technological change and institutional arrangements than is warranted by historical experience. The slavery debates revealed that rapid economic growth and technological change were possible under more than one system of institutions. Which system a society chooses is more an issue of ethics than of economics. The slavery debates revealed that efficient economic institutions may be deeply immoral. They also revealed that economic forces do not automatically select moral solutions. That choice was, and remains, the province of people, not markets.

In many respects the most far-reaching consequence of the antislavery struggle on American civilization was the impetus it gave to the flowering of African American culture. Freedom, even the half freedom of a thwarted reconstruction, made it possible for blacks to develop richly their own forms of self-expression and enterprise: churches, fraternal organizations, movements for political reform, literary circles, newspapers, artistic movements, businesses, and schools. Through these institutions African Americans have not only fundamentally influenced their own society and the whole of American civilization but have also contributed to the shaping of other civilizations around the globe.

A case in point is African American influence on religion domestically and worldwide. In helping to spawn and popularize the Pentecostal and charismatic movements, blacks have contributed to a religious impulse that has embraced some 30,000,000 adherents at home and perhaps an additional 400,000,000 adherents worldwide. Pentecostalism has energized and given hope to the disinherited in impoverished communities, expanded the role of women in church leadership, and promoted a return to a more sensual and mystical religion.

The far-reaching impact of African Americans on contemporary politics is another case in point. There is not only the large role of the black caucus in congressional politics but the role of grass roots black political organizations in promoting diversity as a political imperative to which both of the major political parties have now committed themselves. As a result America is well on the way toward being transformed into a society in which African Americans, Hispanics, Asians, and persons of European ancestry will share in the government of American society. As late as the end of World War II, many thought that such a transformation of American civilization was impossible.

THE IRONY OF THE EARLY DEBATES ABOUT
BLACK STUDIES

When programs in black studies were proposed as a new area of scholarly concentration in the 1960s, there was widespread skepticism. Many scholars feared that black studies would be a "soft field," by which they meant second-rate research in an ill-defined field of study. There were also fears that such programs would become not a field of study but a platform for political infighting by activists in the rising black political movement. Among those scholars who favored an expansion of research into black history and contemporary black socioeconomic issues, many believed that such work should be integrated into the existing academic structure and conducted within already existing departments such as history, sociology, and economics.

As it has turned out, there has been an enormous increase in black studies since the early 1960s, and this development was promoted both by establishing interdisciplinary programs and by devoting more resources to these issues within the traditional departmental structures. This is not to say that the fears of the pessimists were completely unwarranted. Some black studies programs did become a venue for poor work and were disbanded.

Looking back at the early debates about black studies, it is ironic that practically no one recognized that black studies would become a leading arena for the application of the new analytical models and statistical methods of the social sciences. The most ambitious efforts to draw large samples of archival data and transform them into machine-readable form took place during the course of the slavery debates. The applications of econometric techniques to the measurement of demographic and economic processes during these debates preceded similar developments in other fields. Far from being merely another "soft field," black studies became a testing ground for the "hardest" of the new social science methods. Cliometricians working on slavery issues developed new standards for working with large samples of incomplete and biased evidence. These rules and procedures remain an important part of the education of new Ph.D.s in quantitative history and social sciences down to the present, although they have been modified to take account of new techniques made possible by the continuing decline in the cost of processing data and by advances in statistical and social science modeling.

SELECTED BIBLIOGRAPHY

Abzug, Robert H. *Passionate Liberator: Theodore Dwight Weld and the Dilemma of Reform.* New York: Oxford University Press, 1980.

Adams, Alice Dana. *The Neglected Period of Anti-Slavery in America, 1808–1831.* Boston: Ginn, 1908.

Ahlstrom, Sydney E. *A Religious History of the American People.* 2 vols. Garden City, N.J.: Image Books, 1975.

Albanese, Catherine L. *America: Religions and Religion.* Belmont, Calif.: Wadsworth, 1981.

Alexander, Thomas B. *Sectional Stress and Party Strength: A Study of Roll-Call Voting Patterns in the United States House of Representatives, 1836–1860.* Nashville: Vanderbilt University Press, 1967.

Alexander, Thomas B., and Richard E. Beringer. *The Anatomy of the Confederate Congress: A Study of the Influences of Member Characteristics on Legislative Voting Behavior, 1861–1865.* Nashville: Vanderbilt University Press, 1972.

Anderson, Ralph V. "Labor Utilization and Productivity, Diversification and Self-Sufficiency, Southern Plantations, 1800–1840." Ph.D. dissertation, University of North Carolina, Chapel Hill, 1974.

Angle, Paul M., ed. *Created Equal? The Complete Lincoln-Douglas Debates of 1858.* Chicago: University of Chicago Press, 1958.

Anstey, Roger T. "Capitalism and Slavery: A Critique." *Economic History Review* 21 (1968): 307–20.

———. *The Atlantic Slave Trade and British Abolition, 1760–1810.* Atlantic Highlands, N.J.: Humanities Press, 1975.

———. "The Pattern of British Abolitionism in the Eighteenth and Nineteenth Centuries." In *Anti-Slavery, Religion and Reform,* edited by Christine Bolt and Seymour Drescher. Folkestone, U.K.: W. Dawson, 1980.

Bauer, Raymond A., and Alice H. Bauer. "Day to Day Resistance to Slavery." *Journal of Negro History* 27 (1942): 388–419.

Baxter, Jedediah H. *Statistics, Medical and Anthropological, of the Provost-Marshal General's Bureau, Derived from Records of the Examination for Military Service in the Armies of the United States during the Late War of the Rebellion of Over a Million Recruits, Drafted Men, Substitutes, and Enrolled Men.* Washington, D.C., 1875.

Beard, Charles A., and Mary R. Beard. *The Rise of American Civilization.* New ed. New York: Macmillan, 1933.

Bemis, Samuel Flagg. *John Quincy Adams and the Union.* New York: Knopf, 1956.

Benedict, Ruth, and Gene Weltfish. *The Races of Mankind.* New York: Public Affairs Committee (Pamphlet No. 85), 1943.

Benson, Lee. *The Concept of Jacksonian Democracy: New York as a Test Case.* New York: Atheneum, 1961.

Berlin, Ira, and Philip D. Morgan, eds. *The Slaves' Economy: Independent Production by Slaves in the Americas.* London: Frank Cass, 1991.

———. *Cultivation and Culture: Labor and the Shaping of Slave Life in the Americas.* Charlottesville: University Press of Virginia, 1993.

Berry, Thomas Senior. *Western Prices before 1861: A Study of the Cincinnati Market.* Cambridge: Harvard University Press, 1943.

Bertelson, David. *The Lazy South.* New York: Oxford University Press, 1967.

Berthoff, R. T. "Southern Attitudes toward Immigration, 1865–1914." *Journal of Southern History* 17 (1951): 330–60.

Billington, Ray Allen. *The Protestant Crusade, 1800–1860: A Study of the Origins of American Nativism.* Chicago: Quadrangle, 1964.

Blassingame, John W. *The Slave Community: Plantation Life in the Antebellum South.* New York: Oxford University Press, 1972.

———. "Using the Testimony of Ex-Slaves." *Journal of Southern History* 41 (1975): 473–92.

———, ed. *Slave Testimony: Two Centuries of Letters, Speeches, Interviews, and Autobiographies.* Baton Rouge: Louisiana State University Press, 1977.

Boas, Frank. "Anthropology." In *The Encyclopedia of the Social Sciences,* vol. 2. New York: Macmillan, 1930.

Bodo, John R. *The Protestant Clergy and Public Issues, 1812–1848.* Philadelphia: Porcupine, 1980.

Bogue, Allan G. *The Earnest Men: Republicans of the Civil War Senate.* Ithaca: Cornell University Press, 1982.

———. *Clio and the Bitch Goddess: Quantification in American Political History.* Beverly Hills: Sage Publications, 1983.

———. *The Congressman's Civil War.* Cambridge: Cambridge University Press, 1989.

Bolt, Christine, and Seymour Drescher, eds. *Anti-Slavery, Religion, and Reform: Essays in Memory of Roger Anstey.* Folkestone, U.K.: W. Dawson, 1980.

Brady, David W. *Critical Elections and Congressional Policy Making.* Stanford: Stanford University Press, 1988.

Brewer, William M. "Review of *The Peculiar Institution: Slavery in the Ante-Bellum South* by Kenneth M. Stampp." *Journal of Negro History* 57 (1957): 144.

Bridenbaugh, Carl. "The Great Mutation." *American Historical Review* 68 (1963): 315–31.

Burnham, Walter Dean. *Presidential Ballots, 1836–1892.* Baltimore: Johns Hopkins University Press, 1955.

———. "Party Systems and the Political Process." In *The American Party System: Stages of Political Development,* edited by William Nisbet Chambers and Walter Dean Burnham. New York: Oxford University Press, 1967.

———. "The 1980 Earthquake: Realignment: Reactions, or What?" In *The Hidden Election: Politics and Economics in the 1980 Presidential Campaign,* edited by Thomas Ferguson and Joel Rogers. New York: Pantheon, 1981.

———. "Periodization Schemes and 'Party Systems': The 'System of 1896' as a Case in Point." *Social Science History* 10 (1986): 254–314.

———. "Those High Nineteenth-Century American Voting Turnouts: Fact or Fiction?" *Journal of Interdisciplinary History* 16 (1986): 574–644.

———. "Critical Realignment: Dead or Alive?" In *The End of Realignment? Interpreting American Electoral Eras,* edited by Byron E. Shafer. Madison: University of Wisconsin Press, 1991.

Campbell, John. "Work, Pregnancy, and Infant Mortality among Southern Slaves." *Journal of Interdisciplinary History* 14 (1984): 793–812.

———. "As 'A Kind of Freeman'? Slaves' Market-Related Activities in the South Carolina Up Country, 1800–1860." In *Cultivation and Culture: Labor and the Shaping of Slave Life in the Americas,* edited by Ira Berlin and Philip D. Morgan. Charlottesville: University Press of Virginia, 1993.

Cassedy, James H. *Demography in Early America: Beginnings of the Statistical Mind, 1600–1800.* Cambridge: Harvard University Press, 1969.

Clubb, Jerome M., William H. Flanigan, and Nancy H. Zingale. *Partisan Realignment: Voters, Parties, and Government in American History.* Beverly Hills, Calif.: Sage, 1980.

Coclanis, Peter A. "Slavery, African-American Agency, and the World We Have Lost." *Georgia Historical Quarterly* 79 (1995): 873–84.

Cody, Cheryll Ann. "Slave Demography and Family Formation: A Community

Study of the Ball Family Plantations, 1720–1896." Ph.D. dissertation, University of Minnesota, 1982.

Cohn, Raymond L. "Mortality on Immigrant Voyages to New York, 1836–1853." *Journal of Economic History* 44 (1984): 289–300.

———. "Deaths of Slaves in the Middle Passage." *Journal of Economic History* 45 (1985): 685–92.

Cohn, Raymond L., and Richard A. Jensen. "The Determinants of Slave Mortality Rates on the Middle Passage." *Explorations in Economic History* 19 (1982): 269–82.

Cole, Arthur Charles. *The Irrepressible Conflict, 1850–1865.* New York: Macmillan, 1934.

Cole, G. D. H., and Raymond William Postgate. *The Common People, 1746–1946.* 1938. Reprint, London: Methuen, 1976.

Commons, John R. "Horace Greeley and the Working Class Origins of the Republican Party." *Political Science Quarterly* 24 (1909): 468–88.

Commons, John R., et al. *History of Labour in the United States.* 2 vols. New York: Macmillan, 1918.

———, eds. *A Documentary History of American Industrial Society.* 10 vols. Cleveland: Arthur H. Clark Co., 1910.

Conrad, Alfred H., and John R. Meyer. "The Economics of Slavery in the Ante Bellum South." *Journal of Political Economy* 66 (1958): 95–130.

———. *The Economics of Slavery and Other Studies in Econometric History.* 1958. Reprint, Chicago: Aldine, 1964.

Cooper, William J., Jr. *The South and the Politics of Slavery, 1828–1856.* Baton Rouge: Louisiana State University Press, 1978.

Craton, Michael. "Jamaican Slave Mortality: Fresh Light from Worthy Park, Longville, and the Tharp Estates." *Journal of Caribbean History* 3 (1971): 1–27.

———. *Sinews of Empire: A Short History of British Slavery.* Garden City, N.Y.: Anchor Press, 1974.

———. *Searching for the Invisible Man: Slaves and Plantation Life in Jamaica.* Cambridge: Harvard University Press, 1978.

———. "Changing Patterns of Slave Families in the British West Indies." *Journal of Interdisciplinary History* 10 (1979): 1–35.

Crawford, Steven C. "Quantified Memory: A Study of the WPA and Fisk University Slave Narrative Collections." Ph.D. dissertation, University of Chicago, 1980.

———. "Problems in the Quantitative Analysis of the Data Contained in WPA and Fisk University Narratives of Ex-Slaves." In *Without Consent or Contract: The Rise and Fall of American Slavery,* vol. 2, *Evidence and Methods,* edited by Robert William Fogel, Ralph A. Galantine, and Richard L. Manning. New York: W. W. Norton, 1992.

———. "Punishments and Rewards." In *Without Consent or Contract: The Rise and Fall of American Slavery,* vol. 4, *Technical Papers,* vol. 2, *Conditions of Slave Life and the Transition to Freedom,* edited by Robert William Fogel and Stanley L. Engerman. New York: W. W. Norton, 1992.

———. "The Slave Family: A View from the Slave Narratives." In *Strategic Factors in Nineteenth Century American Economic History,* edited by Claudia Goldin and Hugh Rockoff. Chicago: University of Chicago Press, 1992.

Cross, Whitney R. *The Burned-Over District: The Social and Intellectual History of Enthusiastic Religion in Western New York, 1800–1850.* 1950. Reprint, Ithaca: Cornell University Press, 1982.

Curtin, Phillip D. "Epidemiology and the Slave Trade." *Political Science Quarterly* 83 (1968): 190–216.

———. *The Atlantic Slave Trade: A Census.* Madison: University of Wisconsin Press, 1969.

———. "Measuring the Atlantic Slave Trade." In *Race and Slavery in the Western Hemisphere: Quantitative Studies,* edited by Stanley L. Engerman and Eugene D. Genovese. Princeton: Princeton University Press, 1975.

David, Paul A., et al. *Reckoning with Slavery: A Critical Study in the Quantitative History of American Negro Slavery.* New York: Oxford University Press, 1976.

David, Paul A., and Peter Temin. "Capitalist Masters, Bourgeois Slaves." *Journal of Interdisciplinary History* 5 (1975): 445–57.

———. "Explaining the Relative Efficiency of Slave Agriculture in the Antebellum South: Comment." *American Economic Review* 69 (1979): 213–18.

Davis, David Brion. *The Problem of Slavery in Western Culture.* Ithaca: Cornell University Press, 1966.

———. "Slavery and the Post–World War II Historians." *Daedalus* 103 (Spring 1974): 1–16.

———. *The Problem of Slavery in the Age of Revolution, 1770–1823.* Ithaca: Cornell University Press, 1975.

———. *Slavery and Human Progress.* New York: Oxford University Press, 1984.

Davis, Lance E., et al. *American Economic Growth: An Economist's History of the United States.* New York: Harper & Row, 1972.

DeBow, James D. B. *Statistical View of the United States: Compendium of the Seventh Census.* Washington, D.C.: Beverley Tucker, 1854.

———. *The Industrial Resources, Statistics, etc., of the United States, and More Particularly of the Southern and Western States.* 3rd ed. 3 vols. 1854. Reprint, New York: Augustus M. Kelley, 1966.

DeCanio, Stephen J. *Agriculture in the Postbellum South: The Economics of Production and Supply.* Cambridge: MIT Press, 1974.

Degler, Carl N. *Neither Black nor White: Slavery and Race Relations in Brazil and the United States.* New York: Macmillan, 1971.

———. "Experiencing Slavery." *Reviews in American History* 6 (1978): 277–82.

Dillon, Merton L. *The Abolitionists: The Growth of a Dissenting Minority.* New York: W. W. Norton, 1974.

Dodd, William E. *The Cotton Kingdom: A Chronicle of the Old South.* Vol. 27 of *The Chronicles of America.* Edited by Allen Johnson. New Haven: Yale University Press, 1919.

Donald, David Herbert. *Charles Sumner and the Coming of the Civil War.* Chicago: University of Chicago Press, 1960.

Douglass, Frederick. *My Bondage and My Freedom.* 1855. Reprint, New York: Dover Publications, 1969.

Drescher, Seymour. *Econocide: British Slavery in the Era of Abolition.* Pittsburgh: University of Pittsburgh Press, 1977.

———. *Capitalism and Antislavery.* London: Macmillan, 1986.

———. "The Long Goodbye: Dutch Capitalism and Antislavery in Comparative Perspective." *American Historical Review* 99 (1994): 44–69.

Du Bois, W. E. B., ed. *Black Reconstruction in America.* New York: Atheneum, 1970.

———. *The Negro American Family.* 1908. Reprint, Cambridge: MIT Press, 1970.

Dumond, Dwight Lowell. *Antislavery: The Crusade for Freedom in America.* 1961. Reprint, New York: W. W. Norton, 1966.

Dunn, Richard S. *Sugar and Slaves: The Rise of the Planter Class in the British West Indies, 1624–1713.* New York: W. W. Norton, 1973.

Easterlin, Richard A. "Interregional Differences in Per Capita Income, Population, and Total Income, 1840–1950." In *Trends in the American Economy in the Nineteenth Century,* vol. 24 of Studies in Income and Wealth. Princeton: Princeton University Press, 1960.

———. "Regional Income Trends, 1840–1950." In *American Economic History,* edited by Seymour Harris. New York: McGraw-Hill, 1961.

Eaton, Clement. *A History of the Old South.* New York: Macmillan, 1966.

Elkins, Stanley M. *Slavery: A Problem in American Institutional and Intellectual Life.* Chicago: University of Chicago Press, 1959.

———. "The Slavery Debate." *Commentary* 60 (December 1975): 40–54.

Eltis, David. "Nutritional Trends in Africa and the Americas: Heights of Africans, 1819–1839." *Journal of Interdisciplinary History* 12 (1982): 453–75.

———. *Economic Growth and the Ending of the Transatlantic Slave Trade.* New York: Oxford University Press, 1987.

———. "Europeans and the Rise and Fall of African Slavery in the Americas: An Interpretation." *American Historical Review* 98 (1993): 1399–1423.

Engerman, Stanley L. "The Effects of Slavery upon the Southern Economy: A Review of the Recent Debate." *Explorations in Entrepreneurial History* 4 (1967): 71–97.

———. "Slavery and Emancipation in Comparative Perspective: A Look at Some Recent Debates." *Journal of Economic History* 46 (1986): 317–39.

Engerman, Stanley L., et al. "New Directions in Black History." *Forum: A Journal of Social Commentary and the Arts* 1 (1972): 22–41.

Engerman, Stanley L., and Robert E. Gallman. "U.S. Economic Growth, 1783–1860." *Research in Economic History* 8 (1983): 1–46.

Engerman, Stanley L., and Eugene Genovese, eds. *Race and Slavery in the Western Hemisphere: Quantitative Studies.* Princeton: Princeton University Press, 1975.

Escott, Paul D. *Slavery Remembered: A Record of Twentieth-Century Slave Narratives.* Chapel Hill: University of North Carolina Press, 1979.

Evans, Robert, Jr. "The Economics of American Negro Slavery." In *Aspects of Labor Economics.* Princeton: Princeton University Press, 1962.

Fehrenbacher, Don E. *The Dred Scott Case: Its Significance in American Law and Politics.* New York: Oxford University Press, 1978.

———. "The New Political History and the Coming of the Civil War." *Pacific Historical Review* 54 (1985): 117–42.

Field, Alexander James. "Sectoral Shifts in Antebellum Massachusetts: A Reconsideration." *Explorations in Economic History* 15 (1978): 146–71.

Field, Elizabeth B. "Elasticities of Complementarity and Returns to Scale in Antebellum Cotton Agriculture." Ph.D. dissertation, Duke University, 1985.

Fields, Barbara Jeanne. *Slavery and Freedom on the Middle Ground: Maryland during the Nineteenth Century.* New Haven: Yale University Press, 1985.

Finley, M. I. "Slavery." In *International Encyclopedia of the Social Sciences*. Vol. 14. New York: Macmillan, 1968.

―――. *Slavery in Classical Antiquity*. Cambridge: Cambridge University Press, 1968.

―――. *Ancient Slavery and Modern Ideology*. New York: Viking Press, 1980.

Flanders, Ralph B. "Review of *The Peculiar Institution: Slavery in the Ante-Bellum South* by Kenneth M. Stampp." *Mississippi Valley Historical Review* 43 (1957): 679–80.

Fogel, Robert William "From the Marxists to the Mormons." *Times Literary Supplement*, June 13, 1975.

―――. *Without Consent or Contract: The Rise and Fall of American Slavery*. New York: W. W. Norton, 1989.

―――. "Problems in Modeling Complex Dynamic Interactions: The Political Realignment of the 1850s." *Economics and Politics* 4 (1992): 215–54.

―――. "The Quest for the Moral Problem of Slavery: An Historiographic Odyssey." The 33rd Annual Robert Fortenbaugh Memorial Lecture, Gettysburg College, 1994.

Fogel, Robert William, and Stanley L. Engerman. "A Model for the Explanation of Industrial Expansion during the Nineteenth Century: With an Application to the American Iron Industry." *Journal of Political Economy* 77 (1969): 306–28.

―――. *Time on the Cross*. 2 vols. Boston: Little, Brown, 1974.

―――, eds. *The Reinterpretation of American Economic History*. New York: Harper & Row, 1971.

―――, eds. *Without Consent or Contract: The Rise and Fall of American Slavery*. Vol. 3, *Technical Papers*, vol. 1, *Markets and Production*. New York: W. W. Norton, 1992.

―――, eds. *Without Consent or Contract: The Rise and Fall of American Slavery*. Vol. 4, *Technical Papers*, vol. 2, *Conditions of Slave Life and the Transition to Freedom*. New York: W. W. Norton, 1992.

Fogel, Robert William, Stanley L. Engerman, and James Trussell. "Exploring the Uses of Data on Height: The Analysis of Long-Term Trends in Nutrition, Labor Welfare, and Labor Productivity." *Social Science History* 6 (1982): 401–21.

Fogel, Robert William, Ralph A. Galantine, and Richard L. Manning, eds. *Without Consent or Contract: The Rise and Fall of American Slavery*. Vol. 2, *Evidence and Methods*. New York: W. W. Norton, 1992.

Foner, Eric. *Free Soil, Free Labor, Free Men: The Ideology of the Republican Party before the Civil War.* New York: Oxford University Press, 1970.

———. *Politics and Ideology in the Age of the Civil War.* New York: Oxford University Press, 1980.

Foner, Philip S. *Business and Slavery: The New York Merchants and the Irrepressible Conflict.* New York: Russell & Russell, 1968.

Formisano, Ronald P. *The Birth of Mass Political Parties, Michigan, 1827–1861.* Princeton: Princeton University Press, 1971.

———. *Transformation of Political Culture: Massachusetts Parties, 1790s–1840s.* New York: Oxford University Press, 1983.

Foster, Charles I. *An Errand of Mercy: The Evangelical United Front, 1790–1837.* Chapel Hill: University of North Carolina Press, 1960.

Fox-Genovese, Elizabeth. *Within the Plantation Household: Black and White Women of the Old South.* Chapel Hill: University of North Carolina Press, 1988.

Fox-Genovese, Elizabeth, and Eugene D. Genovese. *Fruits of Merchant Capital: Slavery and Bourgeois Property in the Rise and Expansion of Capitalism.* Oxford: Oxford University Press, 1983.

Franklin, John Hope. *The Free Negro in North Carolina, 1790–1860.* Chapel Hill: University of North Carolina Press, 1943.

———. *From Slavery to Freedom: A History of Negro Americans.* 1st and 3rd eds. New York: Knopf, 1947, 1967.

Frazier, E. Franklin. "The Negro Slave Family." *Journal of Negro History* 15 (1930): 198–259.

———. *The Negro Family in the United States.* Chicago: University of Chicago Press, 1939.

Frederickson, George M. *The Black Image in the White Mind: The Debate on Afro-American Character and Destiny, 1817–1914.* New York: Harper & Row, 1971.

Freehling, William W. *Prelude to Civil War: The Nullification Controversy in South Carolina, 1816–1836.* New York: Harper, 1966.

Friedman, Gerald C. "The Heights of Slaves in Trinidad." *Social Science History* 6 (1982): 482–515.

Galenson, David W. *White Servitude in Colonial America: An Economic Analysis.* Cambridge: Cambridge University Press, 1981.

———. *Traders, Planters, and Slaves: Market Behavior in Early English America.* New York: Cambridge University Press, 1986.

Gallman, Robert E. "Commodity Output 1839–1899." In *Trends in the American Economy in the Nineteenth Century*, vol. 24 of Studies in Income and Wealth. Princeton: Princeton University Press, 1960.

————. "Gross National Product in the United States." In *Output, Employment, and Productivity in the United States after 1800*, vol. 30 of Studies in Income and Wealth. New York: Columbia University Press, 1966.

Gates, Paul W. *The Farmer's Age: Agriculture, 1815–1860*. Vol. 3 of *The Economic History of the United States*. New York: Holt, Reinhart, & Winston, 1960.

Gaustad, Edwin Scott. *Historical Atlas of Religion in the United States*. New York: Harper & Row, 1962.

Geggus, David Patrick. *Slavery, War, and Revolution*. Oxford: Clarendon Press, 1982.

Gemery, Henry A., and Jan S. Hogendorn, eds. *The Uncommon Market: Essays in the Economic History of the Atlantic Slave Trade*. New York: Academic Press, 1979.

Genovese, Eugene D. *The Political Economy of Slavery: Studies in the Economy and Society of the Slave South*. New York: Pantheon, 1965.

————. Foreword to Ulrich Bonnell Phillips, *American Negro Slavery: A Survey of the Supply, Employment, and Control of Negro Labor As Determined by the Plantation Regime*. 1st paperback ed. Baton Rouge: Louisiana State University Press, 1966.

————. *The World the Slaveholders Made: Two Essays in Interpretation*. New York: Pantheon, 1969.

————. "American Slaves and Their History: A Special Supplement." *New York Review of Books*, December 3, 1970.

————. *Roll, Jordan, Roll: The World the Slaves Made*. New York: Pantheon, 1974.

————. *From Rebellion to Revolution: Afro-American Slave Revolts in the Making of the Modern World*. Baton Rouge: Louisiana State University Press, 1979.

————. "Western Civilization through Slaveholder Eyes: The Social and Historical Thought of Thomas Roderick Dew." Andrew W. Mellon Lecture, Tulane University, 1986.

Genovese, Eugene D., and Elizabeth Fox-Genovese. "The Religious Ideals of Southern Slave Society." *Georgia Historical Quarterly* 70 (1986): 1–16.

Gienapp, William E. "Nativism and the Creation of a Republican Majority in the North before the Civil War." *Journal of American History* 72 (1985): 529–59.

————. *The Origins of the Republican Party, 1852–1856*. New York: Oxford University Press, 1987.

Goldin, Claudia Dale. *Urban Slavery in the American South, 1820–1860: A Quantitative History.* Chicago: University of Chicago Press, 1976.

Goldin, Claudia Dale, and Kenneth Sokoloff. "Women, Children, and Industrialization in the Early Republic: Evidence from the Manufacturing Censuses." *Journal of Economic History* 42 (1982): 741–74.

———. "The Relative Productivity Hypothesis of Industrialization: The American Case, 1820 to 1850." *Quarterly Journal of Economics* 99 (1984): 461–87.

Gould, B. A. *Investigations in the Military and Anthropological Statistics of American Soldiers.* Cambridge, Mass.: Riverside Press, 1869.

Gray, Lewis Cecil. *History of Agriculture in the Southern United States to 1860.* 2 vols. 1933. Reprint, Gloucester, Mass.: Peter Smith, 1958.

Green, William A. *British Slave Emancipation: The Sugar Colonies and the Great Experiment, 1830–1865.* Oxford: Clarendon Press, 1976.

Greene, Lorenzo J. *The Negro in Colonial New England, 1620–1776.* New York: Columbia University Press, 1942.

Greene, Lorenzo J., and Carter G. Woodson. *The Negro Wage Earner.* Washington, D.C.: Association for the Study of Negro Life and History, 1930.

Greenwood Edition. See George P. Rawick.

Griffin, Clifford S. *Their Brothers' Keepers: Moral Stewardship in the United States, 1800–1865.* New Brunswick, N.J.: Rutgers University Press, 1960.

Griscom, John H. *The Sanitary Condition of the Laboring Class of New York, with Suggestions for Its Improvement.* 1845. Reprint, New York: Arno, 1970.

Grubb, Farley. "Morbidity and Mortality on the North-Atlantic Passage: Eighteenth Century German Immigration." *Journal of Interdisciplinary History* 17 (1987): 565–86.

Gutman, Herbert G. "Persistent Myths about the Afro-American Family." *Journal of Interdisciplinary History* 6 (1975): 181–210.

———. *Slavery and the Numbers Game: A Critique of "Time on the Cross."* Urbana, Ill.: University of Illinois Press, 1975.

———. *The Black Family in Slavery and Freedom, 1750–1925.* New York: Pantheon, 1976.

Hahn, Steven. *The Roots of Southern Populism: Yeoman Farmers and the Transformation of the Georgia Upcountry, 1850–1890.* New York: Oxford University Press, 1983.

Haley, Alex. *Roots.* Garden City, N.Y.: Doubleday, 1976.

Hammond, James Henry. In *Congressional Globe,* 35th Congress, 1st Session, 961–62. 1858.

Hellie, Richard. *Slavery in Russia: 1450–1725.* Chicago: University of Chicago Press, 1982.

———. "Slavery." In *Encyclopedia Britannica,* 15th ed. 1989.

Helper, Hinton Rowan. *The Impending Crisis of the South: How to Meet It.* Edited by George M. Frederickson. 1857. Reprint, Cambridge: Belknap Press, 1968.

Henry, Louis. *Manuel de démographie historique.* Geneva and Paris: Droz, 1967.

———. *On the Measurement of Human Fertility.* Translated and edited by Mindel C. Sheps and Evelyne Lapierre-Adamcyk. New York: Elsevier, 1972.

Herskovits, Melville J. *The Myth of the Negro Past.* 1941. Reprint, Boston: Beacon Press, 1958.

Higman, Barry W. *Slave Population and Economy in Jamaica, 1807–1834.* Cambridge: Cambridge University Press, 1976.

———. *Slave Populations of the British Caribbean, 1807–1834.* Baltimore: Johns Hopkins University Press, 1984.

Hilliard, Sam Bowers. *Hog Meat and Hoecake: Food Supply in the Old South, 1840–1860.* Carbondale, Ill.: Southern Illinois University Press, 1972.

Hofstadter, Richard. "U. B. Phillips and the Plantation Legend." *Journal of Negro History* 29 (1944): 109–24.

———. *The Progressive Historians: Turner, Beard, Parrington.* New York: Knopf, 1968.

———. *The American Political Tradition and the Men Who Made It.* 1948. Reprint, New York: Vintage Books, 1973.

Holt, Michael F. *Forging a Majority: The Formation of the Republican Party in Pittsburgh, 1848–1860.* New Haven: Yale University Press, 1969.

———. "The Antimasonic and Know-Nothing Parties." In *History of U.S. Political Parties,* vol. 1, edited by Arthur Schlesinger. New York: Chelsea House Publishing, 1973.

———. *The Political Crisis of the 1850s.* New York: John Wiley & Sons, 1978.

———. *Political Parties and American Political Development from the Age of Jackson to the Age of Lincoln.* Baton Rouge: Louisiana State University Press, 1992.

———. *The Rise and Fall of the American Whig Party: Jacksonian Politics and the Onset of the Civil War.* New York: Oxford University Press, 1999.

Howe, Daniel Walker. *The Political Culture of the American Whigs.* Chicago: University of Chicago Press, 1979.

Hudson, Larry E., Jr. *To Have and To Hold: Slave Work and Family Life in Antebellum South Carolina.* Athens: University of Georgia Press, 1997.

Huggins, Nathan I. *Black Odyssey: The Afro-American Ordeal in Slavery.* 1977. Reprint, New York: Vintage Books, 1979.

Isley, Jeter Allen. *Horace Greeley and the Republican Party, 1853–1861.* Princeton: Princeton University Press, 1947.

Jensen, Richard J. *The Winning of the Midwest: Social and Political Conflict, 1888–1896.* Chicago: University of Chicago Press, 1971.

———. "Historiography of American Political History." In *Encyclopedia of American Political History: Studies of the Principal Movements and Ideas,* vol. 1, edited by J. P. Greene. New York: Scribner's, 1984.

———. "The Changing Shape of Burnham's Political Universe." *Social Science History* 10 (1986): 209–20.

John, A. Meredith. "The Demography of Slavery in Nineteenth Century Trinidad." Ph.D. dissertation, Princeton University, 1984.

———. *The Plantation Slaves of Trinidad, 1783–1816: A Mathematical and Demographic Inquiry.* Cambridge: Cambridge University Press, 1988.

Jones, Jacqueline. *Labor of Love, Labor of Sorrow: Black Women, Work, and the Family from Slavery to the Present.* New York: Basic Books, 1985.

Jordan, Winthrop D. *White over Black: American Attitudes toward the Negro, 1550–1812.* Chapel Hill: University of North Carolina Press, 1968.

Joyner, Charles. *Down by the Riverside: A South Carolina Slave Community.* Urbana: University of Illinois Press, 1984.

Kelley, Robin D. G. *Race Rebels: Culture, Politics, and the Black Working Class.* New York: Free Press, 1994.

King, Wilma. *Stolen Childhood: Slave Youth in Nineteenth-Century America.* Bloomington: Indiana University Press, 1995.

Kiple, Kenneth F. *The Caribbean Slave: A Biological History.* Cambridge: Cambridge University Press, 1984.

Klein, Herbert S. *Slavery in the Americas: A Comparative Study of Virginia and Cuba.* Chicago: University of Chicago Press, 1967.

———. *The Middle Passage: Comparative Studies in the Atlantic Slave Trade.* Princeton: Princeton University Press, 1978.

———. *African Slavery in Latin America and the Caribbean.* New York: Oxford University Press, 1986.

Kleppner, Paul. *The Cross of Culture: A Social Analysis of Midwestern Politics, 1850–1900.* New York: Free Press, 1970.

———. *The Third Electoral System, 1853–1892: Parties, Voters, and Political Cultures.* Chapel Hill: University of North Carolina Press, 1979.

————. *Who Voted? The Dynamics of Election Turnout, 1870–1980.* New York: Praeger, 1982.

Klingberg, Frank W. "Review of *The Peculiar Institution: Slavery in the Ante-Bellum South* by Kenneth M. Stampp." *American Historical Review* 63 (1957): 139–40.

Knight, Franklin W. *Slave Society in Cuba during the Nineteenth Century.* Madison: University of Wisconsin Press, 1970.

Kousser, J. Morgan. "Ecological Regression and the Analysis of Past Politics." *Journal of Interdisciplinary History* 4 (1973): 237–62.

————. *The Shaping of Southern Politics: Suffrage Restriction and the Establishment of the One-Party South, 1880–1910.* New Haven: Yale University Press, 1974.

————. "The 'New Political History': A Methodological Critique." *Reviews in American History* 4 (1976): 1–14.

————. "Must Historians Regress? An Answer to Lee Benson." *Historical Methods* 19 (1986): 62–81.

Kousser, J. Morgan, and Allan J. Lichtman. "'New Political History': Some Statistical Questions Answered." *Social Science History* 7 (1983): 321–44.

Kraditor, Aileen S. *Means and Ends in American Abolitionism: Garrison and His Critics on Strategy and Tactics, 1834–1850.* 1969. Reprint, New York: Vintage Books, 1970.

Kuznets, Simon. *Seasonal Variations in Industry and Trade.* New York: National Bureau of Economic Research, 1933.

Landes, David S. *The Unbound Prometheus: Technological Change and Industrial Development in Western Europe from 1750 to the Present.* Cambridge: Cambridge University Press, 1969.

————. "On Avoiding Babel." *Journal of Economic History* 37 (1978): 3–12.

Lane, Ann J., ed. *The Debate over Slavery: Stanley Elkins and His Critics.* Urbana: University of Illinois Press, 1971.

Laslett, Peter. *The World We Have Lost: England before the Industrial Age.* 1965. Reprint, New York: Scribner, 1984.

Levine, Lawrence W. *Black Culture and Black Consciousness: Afro-American Folk Thought from Slavery to Freedom.* New York: Oxford University Press, 1977.

Lichtman, Allan J. "Critical Election Theory and the Reality of American Presidential Politics, 1916–40." *American Historical Review* 81 (1976): 317–51.

———. "The End of Realignment Theory? Toward a New Research Program for American Political History." *Historical Methods* 15 (1982): 170–88.

———. "Political Realignment and 'Ethnocultural' Voting in Late Nineteenth-Century America." *Journal of Social History* 16, no. 3 (1983): 55–82.

Littlefield, Daniel C. *Rice and Slaves: Ethnicity and the Slave Trade in Colonial South Carolina.* Baton Rouge: Louisiana State University Press, 1981.

———. *Rice and the Making of South Carolina: An Introductory Essay.* Columbia: South Carolina Department of Archives and History, Public Programs Division, 1995.

MacLeod, Duncan J. *Slavery, Race, and the American Revolution.* London: Cambridge University Press, 1974.

Main, Gloria L. *Tobacco Colony: Life in Early Maryland, 1650–1720.* Princeton: Princeton University Press, 1982.

Malone, Ann Patton. *Sweet Chariot: Slave Family and Household Structure in Nineteenth-Century Louisiana.* Chapel Hill: University of North Carolina Press, 1992.

Malone, Dumas. *The Sage of Monticello.* Vol. 6 of *Jefferson and His Time.* Boston: Little, Brown, 1981.

Margo, Robert A. *Wages and Labor Markets in the United States, 1820–1860.* Chicago: University of Chicago Press, 2000.

Margo, Robert A., and Georgia C. Villaflor. "The Growth of Wages in Antebellum America: New Evidence." *Journal of Economic History* 47 (1987): 873–95.

Marty, Martin E. *Righteous Empire: The Protestant Experience in America.* New York: Dial Press, 1970.

———. *Modern American Religion.* 3 vols. Chicago: University of Chicago Press, 1986–96.

Mathews, Donald G. *Religion in the Old South.* Chicago: University of Chicago Press, 1977.

May, Robert E. *The Southern Dream of a Caribbean Empire, 1854–1861.* Baton Rouge: Louisiana State University Press, 1973.

McCardell, John. *The Idea of a Southern Nation: Southern Nationalists and Southern Nationalism, 1830–1860.* New York: W. W. Norton, 1979.

McCormick, Richard L. *The Party Period and Public Policy: American Politics from the Age of Jackson to the Progressive Era.* New York: Oxford University Press, 1986.

McCormick, Richard P. *The Second American Party System: Party Formation in the Jacksonian Era*. Chapel Hill: University of North Carolina Press, 1966.

McDonald, Roderick A. "Independent Economic Production by Slaves on Antebellum Louisiana Sugar Plantations." In *Cultivation and Culture: Labor and the Shaping of Slave Life in the Americas*, edited by Ira Berlin and Philip D. Morgan. Charlottesville: University Press of Virginia, 1993.

McDonnell, Lawrence T. "Work, Culture, and Society in the Slave South, 1790–1861." In *Black and White Cultural Interaction in the Antebellum South*, edited by Ted Ownby. Jackson: University Press of Mississippi, 1993.

McKitrick, Eric L., ed. *Slavery Defended: The Views of the Old South*. Englewood Cliffs, N.J.: Prentice-Hall, 1965.

McKivigan, John K. *The War against Proslavery Religion: Abolitionism and the Northern Churches, 1830–1865*. Ithaca: Cornell University Press, 1984.

McLoughlin, William G. *Revivals, Awakenings, and Reform: An Essay on Religion and Social Change in America, 1607–1977*. Chicago: University of Chicago Press, 1978.

McMasters, John Bach. *A History of the People of the United States from the Revolution to the Civil War*. 8 vols. New York: D. Appleton and Co., 1883–1913.

McPherson, James M. *Ordeal by Fire: The Civil War and Reconstruction*. New York: Knopf, 1982.

McPherson, James M., et al. *Blacks in America: Bibliographic Essays*. Garden City, N.Y.: Doubleday, 1971.

Meyers, Marvin. *The Jacksonian Persuasion: Politics and Belief*. Stanford: Stanford University Press, 1960.

———. *The Mind of the Founder: Sources of the Political Thought of James Madison*. Rev. ed. Hanover, N.H.: University Press of New England, 1981.

Miers, Suzanne. *Britain and the Ending of the Slave Trade*. New York: Africana Publishing Co., 1975.

Miller, Perry. *The Life of the Mind in America from the Revolution to the Civil War*. San Diego: Harvest, 1965.

Miller, Randall M. "The Man in the Middle: The Black Slave Driver." *American Heritage* 30 (October-November 1979): 40–49.

Mintz, Sidney W. *Caribbean Transformations*. Chicago: Aldine Publishing Co., 1974.

———. "Was the Plantation Slave a Proletarian?" *Review* 2 (1978): 81–98.

———. "Slavery and the Rise of Peasantries." *Historical Reflections* 6 (1979): 213–42.

Mintz, Sidney W., and Douglas Hall. *The Origins of the Jamaican Internal Marketing System.* New Haven: Yale University Press, 1960.

Mokyr, Joel, and N. Eugene Savin. "Some Econometric Problems in the Standard of Living Controversy." *Journal of European Economic History* 7 (1978): 517–25.

Montgomery, David. "The Shuttle and the Cross." *Journal of Social History* 5 (1972): 411–46.

Mooney, Chase C. "Review of *The Peculiar Institution: Slavery in the Ante-Bellum South* by Kenneth M. Stampp." *Journal of Southern History* 22 (1957): 125–28.

Morgan, Edmund S. *American Slavery, American Freedom: The Ordeal of Colonial Virginia.* New York: W. W. Norton, 1975.

Morgan, Philip D. "Work and Culture: The Task System and the World of Lowcountry Blacks, 1700 to 1880." *William and Mary Quarterly* 39 (1982): 563–99.

———. "The Ownership of Property by Slaves in the Mid-Nineteenth-Century Low Country." *Journal of Southern History* 49 (1983): 399–420.

Morris, Richard B. "Review of *The Peculiar Institution: Slavery in the Ante-Bellum South* by Kenneth M. Stampp." *Journal of Economic History* 18 (1958): 89–90.

Morrison, Chaplain W. *Democratic Politics and Sectionalism: The Wilmot Proviso Controversy.* Chapel Hill: University of North Carolina Press, 1967.

Myrdal, Gunnar. *An American Dilemma: The Negro Problem and Modern Democracy.* New York: Harper & Row, 1944.

Nye, Russell Blaine. *Fettered Freedom: Civil Liberties and the Slavery Controversy, 1830–1860.* East Lansing: Michigan State University Press, 1963.

Oakes, James. *The Ruling Race: A History of American Slaveholders.* New York: Knopf, 1982.

———. *Slavery and Freedom: An Interpretation of the Old South.* New York: Knopf, 1990.

Olmsted, Frederick Law. *The Cotton Kingdom: A Traveller's Observations on Cotton and Slavery in the American Slave States. Based upon Three Former Volumes of Journeys and Investigations by the Same Author.* Edited, with an introduction, by Arthur M. Schlesinger. 1953. Reprint, New York: Knopf, Borzoi Books, 1970.

Olson, John F. "The Occupational Structure of Plantation Slave Labor in the Late Antebellum Era." Ph.D. dissertation, University of Rochester, 1983.

Owens, Leslie H. *This Species of Property: Slave Life and Culture in the Old South.* New York: Oxford University Press, 1976.

Owsley, Frank Lawrence. *Plain Folk of the Old South*. Baton Rouge: Louisiana State University Press, 1949.

Parish, Peter J. *Slavery: History and Historians*. New York: Harper & Row, 1989.

Parker, William N., ed. *The Structure of the Cotton Economy of the Antebellum South*. Washington, D.C.: Agricultural History Society, 1970.

Parrington, Vernon Louis. *Main Currents in American Thought: An Interpretation of American Literature from the Beginnings to 1920*. Vol. 2, *1800–1860*. New York: Harcourt, Brace, and Co., 1930.

Patterson, Orlando. *The Sociology of Slavery*. New York: Academic Press, 1972.

———. *Slavery and Social Death: A Comparative Study*. Cambridge: Harvard University Press, 1982.

Penningroth, Dylan. "Slavery, Freedom, and Social Claims to Property among African Americans in Liberty County, Georgia, 1850–1880." *Journal of American History* 84 (1997): 405–35.

Perry, Lewis. *Radical Abolitionism: Anarchy and the Government of God in Antislavery Thought*. Ithaca: Cornell University Press, 1973.

Pessen, Edward. *Jacksonian America: Society, Personality, and Politics*. Homewood, Ill.: Dorsey, 1978.

Phillips, Ulrich Bonnell. *A History of Transportation in the Eastern Cotton Belt to 1860*. New York: Columbia University Press, 1908.

———. *American Negro Slavery: A Survey of the Supply, Employment, and Control of Negro Labor As Determined by the Plantation Regime*. 1918. Reprint, Baton Rouge: Louisiana State University Press, 1966.

———, ed. *Plantation and Frontier Documents, 1649–1863*. Vols. 1 and 2 of *A Documentary History of American Industrial Society*, edited by John R. Commons et al. Cleveland: A. H. Clark Co., 1910.

Postell, William D. *The Health of Slaves on Southern Plantations*. 1951. Reprint, Gloucester, Mass.: Peter Smith, 1970.

Potter, David M. *The Impending Crisis, 1848–1861*. New York: Harper, 1976.

Pressly, Thomas J. *Americans Interpret Their Civil War*. Princeton: Princeton University Press, 1954.

Quarles, Benjamin. *Black Abolitionists*. New York: Oxford University Press, 1969.

Ragatz, Lowell J. *The Fall of the Planter Class in the British Caribbean, 1763–1833: A Study in Social and Economic History*. New York: Century Co., 1928.

Ramsdell, Charles W. "The Natural Limits of Slavery Expansion." *Mississippi Valley Historical Review* 16 (1929): 151–71.

Ransom, Roger L. *Conflict and Compromise: The Political Economy of Slavery, Emancipation, and the American Civil War.* Cambridge: Cambridge University Press, 1989.

Ransom, Roger L., and Richard Sutch. *One Kind of Freedom: The Economic Consequences of Emancipation.* Cambridge: Cambridge University Press, 1977.

Rawick, George P., ed. *The American Slave: A Composite Autobiography.* 19 vols. Contributions in Afro-American Studies, No. 11. Westport, Conn.: Greenwood Press, 1972.

Rhodes, James Ford. *History of the United States from the Compromise of 1850.* Vol. 1, *1850–1854.* 1893. Reprint, New York: Macmillan, 1928.

Savitt, Todd L. *Medicine and Slavery: The Diseases and Health Care of Blacks in Antebellum Virginia.* Urbana: University of Illinois Press, 1978.

Scarborough, William K. *The Overseer: Plantation Management in the Old South.* Baton Rouge: Louisiana State University Press, 1966.

Schaefer, Donald F. "Yeoman Farmers and Economic Democracy: A Study of Wealth and Economic Mobility in the Western Tobacco Region, 1850 to 1860." *Explorations in Economic History* 15 (1978): 421–37.

———. "A Statistical Profile of Frontier and New South Migration: 1850–1860." *Agricultural History* 59 (1985): 563–78.

Schlesinger, Arthur Meier. *The Rise of the City, 1878–1898.* New York: Macmillan, 1933.

Schlesinger, Arthur M., Jr., "The Causes of the Civil War: A Note on Historical Sentimentalism." *Partisan Review* 16 (1949): 969–81.

———, ed. *History of the U.S. Political Parties.* Vol. 1. New York: Chelsea House Publishing, 1973.

Schmitz, Mark. "Economic Analysis of Antebellum Sugar Plantations in Louisiana." Ph.D. dissertation, University of North Carolina at Chapel Hill, 1974.

Schwartz, Marie Jenkins. "One Thing Then Another: Slave Children's Labor in Alabama." *Labor's Heritage* 7 (Winter 1996): 22–33, 56–57.

Sewell, Richard H. *John P. Hale and the Politics of Abolition.* Cambridge: Harvard University Press, 1965.

———. *Ballots for Freedom: Antislavery Politics in the United States, 1837–1860.* New York: Oxford University Press, 1976.

Sheridan, Richard B. *Sugar and Slavery: An Economic History of the British West Indies, 1623–1775.* Aylesbury, U.K.: Ginn and Co., 1974.

————. *Doctors and Slaves: A Medical and Demographic History of Slavery in the British West Indies, 1680–1834.* Cambridge: Cambridge University Press, 1985.

Silbey, Joel H. *The Shrine of Party: Congressional Voting Behavior, 1841–1852.* Pittsburgh: University of Pittsburgh Press, 1967.

————. *A Respectable Minority: The Democratic Party in the Civil War Era, 1860–1868.* New York: W. W. Norton, 1977.

————. *The Partisan Imperative: The Dynamics of American Politics before the Civil War.* New York: Oxford University Press, 1985.

————. *The American Political Nation, 1838–1893.* Stanford: Stanford University Press, 1991.

————. "Beyond Realignment and Realignment Theory: American Political Eras, 1789–1989." In *The End of Realignment? Interpreting American Electoral Eras,* edited by Byron E. Shafer. Madison: University of Wisconsin Press, 1991.

Smillie, Wilson G. *Public Health: Its Promise for the Future.* New York: Macmillan, 1955.

Smith, H. Shelton. *In His Image, but . . . : Racism in Southern Religion, 1780–1910.* Durham, N.C.: Duke University Press, 1972.

Smith, Mark M. "Old South Time in Comparative Perspective." *American Historical Review* 101 (1996): 1432–69.

————. "Time, Slavery, and Plantation Capitalism in the Ante-bellum American South." *Past and Present* 150 (1996): 142–68.

————. *Mastered by the Clock: Time, Slavery, and Freedom in the American South.* Chapel Hill: University of North Carolina Press, 1997.

————. *Debating Slavery: Economy and Society in the Antebellum American South.* Cambridge: Cambridge University Press, 1998.

Smith, Timothy L. *Revivalism and Social Reform in Mid-Nineteenth-Century America.* New York: Abingdon, 1957.

Smith, Walter Buckingham, and Arthur Harrison Cole. *Fluctuations in American Business, 1790–1860.* Cambridge: Harvard University Press, 1935.

Snow, C. P. *The Two Cultures and the Scientific Revolution.* New York: Cambridge University Press, 1959.

Sokoloff, Kenneth L. "Industrialization and the Growth of the Manufacturing Sector in the Northeast, 1820–1850." Ph.D. dissertation, Harvard University, 1982.

————. "Was the Transition from the Artisanal Shop to the Nonmechanized Factory Associated with Gains in Efficiency? Evidence from the U.S. Manufacturing Censuses of 1820 and 1850." *Explorations in Economic History* 21 (1984): 351–82.

———. "Productivity Growth in Manufacturing during Early Industrialization: Evidence from the American Northeast, 1820–1860." In *Long-Term Factors in American Economic Growth,* edited by Stanley Engerman and Robert Gallman, vol. 51 of Studies in Income and Wealth. Chicago: University of Chicago Press, 1986.

Solow, Barbara L., and Stanley L. Engerman, eds. *British Capitalism and Caribbean Slavery: The Legacy of Eric Williams.* Cambridge: Cambridge University Press, 1987.

Soltow, Lee. "Economic Inequality in the United States in the Period from 1790 to 1860." *Journal of Economic History* 31 (1971): 822–39.

———. *Men and Wealth in the United States, 1850–1870.* New Haven: Yale University Press, 1975.

Stampp, Kenneth M. *And the War Came: The North and the Secession Crisis, 1860–1861.* Baton Rouge: Louisiana State University Press, 1950.

———. "The Historian and Southern Negro Slavery." *American Historical Review* 57 (1952): 618–24.

———. *The Peculiar Institution: Slavery in the Ante-bellum South.* New York: Knopf, 1956.

———. "Rebels and Sambos: The Search for the Negro's Personality in Slavery." *Journal of Southern History* 37 (1971): 367–92.

Starobin, Robert S. *Industrial Slavery in the Old South.* New York: Oxford University Press, 1970.

Steckel, Richard H. "Miscegenation and the American Slave Schedules." *Journal of Interdisciplinary History* 11 (1980): 251–63.

———. *The Economics of U.S. Slave and Southern White Fertility.* New York: Garland Publishing, 1985.

———. "A Peculiar Population: The Nutrition, Health, and Mortality of American Slaves from Childhood to Maturity." *Journal of Economic History* 46 (1986): 721–41.

Stevenson, Brenda E. *Life in Black and White: Family and Community in the Slave South.* New York: Oxford University Press, 1996.

Stone, Lawrence. "History and the Social Sciences in the Twentieth Century." In *The Future of History: Essays in the Vanderbilt University Centennial Symposium,* edited by Charles F. Delzell. Nashville: Vanderbilt University Press, 1977.

Stuckey, Sterling. "Through the Prism of Folklore: The Black Ethos in Slavery." In *American Negro Slavery*, 2nd. ed., edited by Allen Weinstein and Frank Otto Gatell. New York: Oxford University Press, 1973.

————. *Slave Culture: Nationalist Theory and the Foundations of Black America*. New York: Oxford University Press, 1987.

Sutch, Richard. "The Breeding of Slaves for Sale and the Westward Expansion of Slavery, 1850–1860." In *Race and Slavery in the Western Hemisphere: Quantitative Studies*, edited by Stanley L. Engerman and Eugene Genovese. Princeton: Princeton University Press, 1975.

Swan, Dale E. "The Structure and Profitability of the Antebellum Rice Industry, 1859." Ph.D. dissertation, University of North Carolina, 1972.

Swieringa, Robert P. "Religion and Political Behavior in the Nineteenth Century: Voting, Values, Cultures." Presented at the Conference on Religion and American Politics, Institute for the Study of American Evangelicals, Wheaton, Ill., March 18, 1988.

Sydnor, Charles S. *Slavery in Mississippi.* 1933. Reprint, Gloucester, Mass.: P. Smith, 1965.

Takaki, Ronald T. *A Pro-Slavery Crusade: The Agitation to Reopen the African Slave Trade.* New York: Free Press, 1971.

Temin, Peter. *Iron and Steel in Nineteenth-Century America: An Economic Inquiry.* Cambridge: MIT Press, 1963.

————. *The Jacksonian Economy.* New York: W. W. Norton, 1969.

Temperley, Howard. *British Antislavery, 1833–1870.* Columbia, S.C.: University of South Carolina Press, 1972.

————. "Capitalism, Slavery, and Ideology." *Past and Present* 75 (1977): 94–118.

Thomas, John L. *The Liberator, William Lloyd Garrison: A Biography.* Boston: Little, Brown, 1963.

————, ed. *Slavery Attacked: The Abolitionist Crusade.* Englewood Cliffs, N.J.: Prentice-Hall, 1965.

Thompson, Edward P. "Time, Work-Discipline, and Industrial Capitalism." *Past and Present* 38 (1967), 56–97.

————. *The Making of the English Working Class.* Middlesex, U.K.: Penguin Books, 1975.

Thornton, J. Mills, III. *Politics and Power in a Slave Society: Alabama, 1800–1860.* Baton Rouge: Louisiana State University Press, 1978.

Thorp, William Long. *Business Annals.* New York: National Bureau of Economic Research, 1926.

Trent, William P. *William Gilmore Simms*. Boston: Houghton Mifflin, 1892.

Trussell, James, and Richard Steckel. "The Age of Slaves at Menarche and Their First Birth." *Journal of Interdisciplinary History* 8 (1978): 477–505.

Tucker, George. *Progress of the United States in Population and Wealth in Fifty Years, As Exhibited by the Decennial Census*. New York: Press of Hunt's Merchants' Magazine, 1843.

Tulloch, A. M. "On the Sickness and Mortality among the Troops in the West Indies," pts. 1–3. *Journal of the Statistical Society of London* 1 (1838): 129–42, 216–30, 428–43.

Turner, Frederick Jackson. *The Frontier in American History*. New York: H. Holt and Co., 1921.

Van den Boogaart, E., and P. C. Emmer. "Plantation Slavery in Surinam in the Last Decade before Emancipation: The Case of Catherine Sophie." In *Comparative Perspectives on Slavery in New World Plantation Societies*, edited by Vera Rubin and Arthur Tuden. New York: New York Academy of Sciences, 1977.

Van Deusen, Glyndon G. *Thurlow Weed, Wizard of the Lobby*. Boston: Little, Brown, 1947.

———. *Horace Greeley, Nineteenth-Century Crusader*. 1953. Reprint, New York: Hill and Wang, 1964.

———. *The Jacksonian Era, 1828–1848*. 1959. Reprint, New York: Harper, 1963.

———. *William Henry Seward*. New York: Oxford University Press, 1967.

Wade, Richard C. *Slavery in the Cities: The South, 1820–1860*. New York: Oxford University Press, 1964.

Wahl, Jenny Bourne. "New Results on the Decline in Household Fertility in the United States from 1750 to 1900." In *Long-Term Factors in American Economic Growth*, edited by Stanley L. Engerman and Robert E. Gallman, vol. 51 of Studies in Income and Wealth. Chicago: University of Chicago Press (for NBER), 1986.

Walsh, Lorena Seebach. "Charles County, Maryland, 1658–1705: A Study of Chesapeake Social and Political Structure." Ph.D. dissertation, Michigan State University, 1977.

Walters, Ronald G. *The Antislavery Appeal: American Abolitionism after 1830*. Baltimore: Johns Hopkins University Press, 1976.

Walvin, James. "The Public Campaign in England against Slavery, 1787–1834." In *The Abolition of the Atlantic Slave Trade*, edited by David Eltis and James Wade. Madison: University of Wisconsin Press, 1981.

Webber, Thomas. *Deep like the Rivers: Education in the Slave Quarter Community, 1831–1865.* New York: W. W. Norton, 1978.

Weld, Theodore Dwight. *American Slavery As It Is: Testimony of a Thousand Witnesses.* New York: American Anti-Slavery Society, 1839.

Wells, Robert V. *The Population of the British Colonies in America before 1776.* Princeton: Princeton University Press, 1975.

Wesley, Charles H. *Negro Labor in the United States, 1850–1925: A Study in American Economic History.* New York: Vanguard Press, 1927.

Whaples, Robert. "Where Is There Consensus among American Economic Historians?" *Journal of Economic History* 55 (1995): 139–54.

Wilentz, Sean. *Chants Democratic: New York City and the Rise of the American Working Class, 1788–1850.* New York: Oxford University Press, 1984.

Williams, Eric. *Capitalism and Slavery.* 1944. Reprint, New York: Capricorn Books, 1966.

Wiltse, Charles M. *John C. Calhoun.* 3 vols. Indianapolis: Bobbs-Merrill, 1944–51.

Woodman, Harold D. *King Cotton and His Retainers.* Lexington, Ky.: University of Kentucky Press, 1968.

Woodson, Carter G. *The Education of the Negro Prior to 1861: A History of the Education of the Colored People of the United States from the Beginning of Slavery to the Civil War.* 2nd ed. Washington, D.C.: Associated Publishers, 1919.

———. *The History of the Negro Church.* Washington, D.C.: Associated Publishers, 1921.

———. *Free Negro Heads of Families in the United States in 1830 Together with a Brief Treatment of the Free Negro.* Washington, D.C.: Association for the Study of Negro Life and History, 1925.

———. *The Negro in Our History.* 3rd and 4th eds. Washington, D.C.: Associated Publishers, 1927, 1931.

———, ed. *The Mind of the Negro As Reflected in Letters Written during the Crisis, 1800–1860.* Washington, D.C.: Association for the Study of Negro Life and History, 1926.

Woodward, C. Vann. *The Burden of Southern History.* 1960. Reprint, Baton Rouge: Louisiana State University Press, 1968.

———. "History and the Third Culture." *Journal of Contemporary History* 3 (1968): 23–35.

———. *American Counterpoint: Slavery and Racism in the North-South Dialogue.* Boston: Little, Brown, 1971.

Wright, Gavin. "The Economics of Cotton in the Antebellum South." Ph.D. dissertation, Yale University, 1969.

———. *Political Economy of the Cotton South: Households, Markets, and Wealth in the Nineteenth Century.* New York: W. W. Norton, 1978.

———. *Old South, New South: Revolutions in the Southern Economy since the Civil War.* New York: Basic Books, 1986.

Wrigley, E. A., and R. S. Schofield. *The Population History of England, 1541–1871: A Reconstruction.* Cambridge: Harvard University Press, 1981.

Wyatt-Brown, Bertram. *Lewis Tappan and the Evangelical War against Slavery.* Cleveland: Press of Case Western Reserve University, 1969.

———. *Southern Honor: Ethics and Behavior in the Old South.* New York: Oxford University Press, 1982.

Yang, Donghyu. "Aspects of United States Agriculture circa 1860." Ph.D. dissertation, Harvard University, 1984.

———. "The Parker-Gallman Sample and Wealth Distributions for the Antebellum South: A Reply." *Explorations in Economic History* 22 (1985): 227–31.

Yasuba, Yasukichi. "The Profitability and Viability of Plantation Slavery in the United States." *Economic Studies Quarterly* 12 (1961): 6067.

Zilversmit, Arthur. *The First Emancipation: The Abolition of Slavery in the North.* Chicago: University of Chicago Press, 1967.

INDEX